GW00383292

THE CONDITION OF BRIT.

THE CONDITION
OF BRITAIN

Essays on Frederick Engels

Edited by JOHN LEA and GEOFF PILLING

Pluto Press
LONDON • EAST HAVEN, CT

First published 1996 by Pluto Press
345 Archway Road, London N6 5AA and
140 Commerce Street, East Haven, CT 06512, USA

British Library Cataloguing in Publication Data
A catalogue record for this book is available from the British Library

ISBN 0 7453 0962 3 hbk

Library of Congress Cataloging in Publication Data
The condition of Britain / edited by John Lea and Geoff Pilling.
      p.   cm.
   Includes bibliographical references and index.
   ISBN 0-7453-0962-3 (hbk)
    1. Working class—Great Britain, 2. Great Britain—Economic
conditions—1993–   3. Great Britain—Social conditions—1945–
4. Engels, Frederick, 1820–1865. Die Lage der argeitenden Klasse in
England.   I. Lea, John.   II. Pilling, Geoffrey.
HD8391.C585 1995
306'.0941—dc20   95-37975
                                         CIP

Designed, typeset and produced for Pluto Press by
Chase Production Services, Chipping Norton, OX7 5QR
Printed in the EC by WSOY, Finland

Contents

Notes on Contributors

PETER FRYER is a freelance writer living in London. He is the author of several books, including *Staying Power* and *Black People in the British Empire* (both published by Pluto Press).

KEITH GIBBARD teaches economics at Manchester Metropolitan University where he specialises in classical and Marxist political economy.

JOHN LEA teaches at Middlesex University. His books include *What Is To Be Done About Law and Order?* (with Jock Young). He has recently translated from Italian *Limited Responsibilities* by Tamar Pitch.

DORIA PILLING is Research Fellow at City University, London. She is author of several books, including *Escape from Disadvantage*, and has recently edited, with Graham Watson, *Evaluating Quality in Services for Disabled and Older People*.

GEOFF PILLING teaches at Middlesex University. His books include *Marx's Capital: Philosophy and Political Economy* and *The Crisis of Keynesian Economics*.

CLIFF SLAUGHTER formerly taught at the University of Bradford. His books include *Marxism and the Class Struggle* and *Marxism, Sociology and Literature*.

Note

All references to the Marx–Engels *Collected Works*, Moscow, 1975, are as follows:

4: 320, meaning vol. 4, p. 320.

References to the *Collected Works of V. I. Lenin* are as follows:

LCW, followed by the volume number, thus: *LCW* 14.

It should be noted that the views expressed in each chapter are those of the author concerned, and not necessarily those of the editors.

Introduction

John Lea and Geoff Pilling

THE YEAR 1995 marks the hundredth anniversary of the death of Frederick Engels. The text for which he is above all remembered is *The Condition of the Working Class in England*, one of the founding documents of the materialist conception of history. While Marx came to materialism and communism principally through his critique of classical German philosophy and the analysis of the political and economic conditions of backward Germany, Engels was able to make a study of the most developed capitalist country of that time and moved towards socialism under the influence of Chartism and Owen's utopian socialism.

First published in 1845 and written by Engels as a young man of 24 working in his father's textile firm in Manchester, it reveals, some 20 years before the appearance of Marx's *Capital*, that splendid blend of detailed empirical study and theoretical clarity which was to become the hallmark of classical Marxism, long before the Epigones laboured to turn Marxism into arid conceptual gameplay and authoritarian political dogma and practice.

This in itself would be reason enough for a rereading, particularly in an age when the social sciences continually present us with a choice between mindless empiricism and vacuous theoretical formalism. But, more than this, 150 years after it was written, *The Condition* sounds more in tune with our times than texts on the 'social structure of advanced industrial society' written a mere 20 years ago and now gathering dust on library shelves. We are living through a period of fundamental social and political upheaval and it is at such times that the past suddenly becomes nearer and more relevant. It has become a commonplace that the material conditions of life in Britain for growing numbers of people – the young, the homeless, and women in particular – are beginning to move in the direction of those described in Engels's Manchester of the 1840s.

Just as Engels knew that the processes he was describing in that city 150 years ago were of world significance, so today poverty is a major global problem. The United Nations *World Economic Survey* for

1

1993 reveals that one in five of the planet's population live in poverty (defined as an income below $275 per year). After decades of 'development plans', 'aid programmes' and the like, the report documents the rapid growth of poverty in the colonial and semi-colonial countries, but also its sharp increase in the advanced capitalist countries. In North America and Western Europe an average of one person in six now lives below the poverty line. Poverty grows along with unemployment; however, today unemployment is no longer simply that produced by the trade cycle – an important feature of Engels's book – but is increasingly of a structural and long-term character. In this respect the situation has gone beyond the conditions so vividly described by Engels. More and more of the unemployed no longer constitute part of a 'reserve army', awaiting an upturn in the trade cycle to be drawn back into the labour force: they are now permanently unemployed, with no prospect or hope of work.[1]

In the growing debate on poverty and inequality in Britain, Engels's work has, as Doria Pilling shows in Chapter 1, moved firmly back on to the agenda, not only from the standpoint of actual living conditions but as an important rebuff to the right wing's attempt to blame the poor for their own predicament. The return to Lady Thatcher's 'Victorian values' means a return to Blake's 'dark satanic mills' – though with most of the mills now closed. Engels speaks directly to these issues – growing poverty and immiseration and the necessity for fundamental social change – which now confront working people in Britain and throughout the world; and they do so as their traditional party for the last 90 years and more, the Labour Party, makes crystal clear that it has now openly renounced any idea of such change. Engels was able to draw the conclusions that he did because the development of British capitalism was archetypal for capitalism as a whole, and not some local peculiarity. Manchester in the 1840s was not simply a city in northern England: it represented the highest point of the development of the capitalist mode of production, graphically anticipating the dynamics and contradictions of its development. Likewise 'the decline of Britain' is not today a local peculiarity expressing some idiosyncratic 'backwardness' derived from the lack of a thoroughgoing bourgeois revolution or the untoward dominance of financial over industrial capital, as certain radicals suggest. As Keith Gibbard documents in Chapter 2, the decline of the British economy holds up a mirror to the rest of the capitalist world, as surely as capitalist Britain did in the middle of the last century. Insofar as Britain is dominated by a handful of bankers, 'money-men' and sundry others type of speculator, it reflects, in concentrated form, conditions in the world as a whole.

In another respect also history now repeats itself. Engels wrote his classic study at just that point where Britain assumed world dominance, controlling an Empire 'on which the sun never set and wages rarely rose'. It was on the basis of the lead taken by Britain that the rest of the world began the process of capitalist industrialisation, a process usually financed with British money. In short, it was Britain, with Manchester at its centre, that brought the world market into being. But if history repeats itself, it does so in an upside-down manner. For just as 150 years ago Britain was dragging a world market into being, so now today it is, as Gibbard suggests, the contradictions of this very world system that are threatening to turn what has been a long-drawn-out period of relative decline for British capital into an absolute one. In short it is what is now fashionably called the 'globalisation' of capital that is undermining the ability of the British ruling class any longer to pursue an independent economic or political strategy on the world arena. Here, to take one example, lies the source of the deep divisions in the British establishment about its orientation towards Europe.

Engels talks about poverty and immiseration in *The Condition* in a way that is central to the nature of the materialist conception of history. He was not documenting the consequences of an 'industrial revolution' – conceived of as simply factory production and urban living – but analysing the contradictory social relations of capitalism: of the formation of the working class as the essence of the productive forces of capitalism and at the same time the potential agent of capitalism's destruction. As Geoff Pilling demonstrates in Chapter 3, debates among economic historians as to precisely when, or indeed whether, the industrial revolution took place are generally characterised by a one-sided empiricism mesmerised by the issue of technology. Engels saw the industrial revolution as a social process, having at its core the creation of a quite new phenomenon, the modern industrial working class. For him it was a profoundly contradictory turning point in world history, both imposing misery and degradation on the working class but, by virtue of the very creation of such a class, laying the basis for a newer, truly human form of society. Pilling criticises those economic historians who, having reduced the 'industrial revolution' largely to technology, thereby claimed that it is not a distinguishable, qualitative, historical event. By implication such a critique extends to those theorists – including not a few ex-Marxists – who have in recent years announced a fundamentally new stage in the development of capitalism brought about, for example, by information technology, which magically overcomes the fundamental antagonisms between capital and labour intrinsic to the social relations of capitalism.

Thus Engels cannot be read as simply a documentation of the condition of the working class as merely the sufferer of poverty and immiseration, real those these things were (and increasingly are). Even the existence of poverty has to be understood dialectically. In early capitalism the accumulation of capital depended on low wages and the maximisation of the working day, that is it involved, as its main feature, the extraction of surplus value in its absolute form. Here again, we can say that the situation that Engels describes now returns: one of the central features of the strategy of the government for the last decade and a half has been to create the conditions – largely to be brought about by the break-up of the trade unions – where control over hours, working conditions and safety at work has been steadily eroded.

The brutalisation of the working class Engels graphically portrays. But, as he was among the first to realise, the accumulation of capital is the motive force creating the conditions in which the working class can develop organisation, the strength to resist and, eventually, replace capitalism with a more just society. These developments, as John Lea shows in Chapter 4, lie behind Engels's view of working-class crime. He sees crime not simply as the result of the demoralisation and brutalisation of the working class by capitalism – though even this would have represented an advance on the positivism and search for criminogenic character defects still peddled today by conservative criminology – but also, paradoxically, the starting point for resistance to capitalism. Out of the rage and destructive individual violence of crime, from the machine-smashing mobs of the early nineteenth century onwards, came the development of working-class political consciousness that reached its high point in the Chartist movement of the 1840s. Here again the emergence of Chartism had implications that extended far beyond these shores; for 'Britain gave the world Chartism, the first broad, truly mass and politically organised proletarian revolutionary movement.'[2]

But if such issues as poverty and criminality have to be seen in the context of the growth of the working class in opposition to capital, the 'same' phenomena have to be looked at in the very different context of capitalism's decline in the present epoch. Poverty as the precursor to the further development of the productive forces of capitalism is one thing; poverty resulting from the fact that capitalism today can deploy the most modern technology only to further the process of global immiseration, the impoverishment of countless millions and the general destruction of humanity's productive forces is quite something else. (The world-wide threat to the environment posed by capitalism today transcends anything that Engels saw in Manchester and its surrounding filthy, smoke-polluted towns.) Likewise, crime as a stage in the development of class consciousness is different from crime as a result of the decay left by a capitalism that is no longer capable of developing society, but only of tearing it apart. Capitalism no longer develops society and it no longer develops the working class. But the latter does not need to go through all the stages of political development and repeat the processes documented by Engels. The working class, internationally, has the capacity to act to stop the destruction being wrought by global capitalism. And the conditions for it doing so are becoming more rather than less favourable.

This is the paradox noted by Cliff Slaughter in Chapter 5. The collapse of the Stalinist regimes of the USSR and Eastern Europe was initially heralded as the 'victory of capitalism'. Now the celebration is over as it is gradually dawning on even the dimmest representative of the ruling class that not only is capitalism incapable of effecting a smooth process of reclamation of the former 'communist' countries but that the removal of the theoretical and political shackles of Stalinism liberates new forces in the political development of the international working class. The consolidation and education of these new forces requires, Slaughter argues, a major work of excavation. Engels must be recovered from the rubble of Stalinism, understood not simply as a brutal system of oppression of the working class but as a theoretical onslaught on Marxism that threatened to turn it completely into a barren mechanical determinism. Yet the greatest damage inflicted by Stalinism was the blows it struck at working-class consciousness. In the fight for the recovery of such consciousness, Engels's book is of the greatest value, having at its centre a conception of the working class, not as a series of individuals but as a force, a movement, brought into being by the development of capital itself. Here lay Engels's decisive advance, for, as Slaughter shows, even the most trenchant critics of the bourgeois order, such as Thomas Carlyle, failed to understand the nature of the working class, failed to grasp the significance of the struggles in which it was engaged or to comprehend the nature of the consciousness that was developing within it, and failed to understand this newly emerging working class as the real 'critic' of capitalism.

In Chapter 6 Peter Fryer draws attention to the fact that Engels was a 'man of his time' with many of the attitudes and views of mid-Victorian Britain. He documents the fact that both Engels and Marx in several respects shared the standpoint of many of their contemporaries in their attitude to the family, to the Irish, to Jews, etc. It should be noted though that there are several indications of Engels moving to a more perceptive view of the family and even perhaps in relation to the Irish (see Chapter 1). But while painting Engels 'warts and all', Fryer stresses that this in no way vitiates the scientific merits of his work, so brilliantly demonstrated in *The Condition*.

In this way Fryer demonstrates a fundamental difference between Marxism and any notion that knowledge is one-sidedly reducible to, or simply a passive expression of, either the personal identities of its authors or the social conditions in which they write. The development of the materialist conception of history was, of course, only possible under capitalism, and presupposed all the social and intellectual conquests of previous historical periods. But, by grasping the dialectic inherent in capitalism itself, historical materialism both reflects and goes beyond that system, providing the key to its supercession, a process which includes changes in the personal lives and attitudes of individuals.

The remarkable thing therefore is not so much that Engels, understandably, was limited by his day and age, but the extent to which he saw beyond it. The 'Condition of England' question was one exercising the minds of many writers and critics: for example, Charles Dickens, *Hard Times* (1854); Elizabeth Gaskell, *Mary Barton* (1848); and Charles Kingsley, *Alton Locke* (1850). But none came anywhere near to Engels in their appreciation of the historic significance of what was happening in Manchester, a city of some 400,000 inhabitants in a small island off the coast of continental Europe. For Engels did not simply describe the poverty and squalor that he saw all around him. Nor did he merely draw some general conclusions from the facts he so vividly and movingly points to in *The Condition*. He was able to see into the future, transcending the limits of his time, because of the theoretical conquests he had already made before he set foot in Manchester. The critique of political economy, although not yet completed, was under way[3] and, as Slaughter points out, already in *The Holy Family*, the first joint effort of Marx and Engels and one that appeared before *The Condition*, the revolutionary character of the working class had been established. It was in the former work that Marx and Engels settled accounts with the 'critical critics' who had condemned the working class as an 'uncritical mass'. So Engels saw the facts of poverty, misery and starvation that surrounded him on his tours of the northern towns through eyes that were already theoretically well educated. And yet there is no doubt that his experiences in Manchester had a profound impact on him, marking a decisive step in his development towards revolutionary socialism. ('It was not until he came to England that Engels became a socialist', claimed Lenin.[4]) He arrived at his conclusions about the historical character of the working class, not on the basis of searching for the features common to the working-class movement in each country – it would hardly be an exaggeration to say that at this stage a developed working-class movement existed only in England – but by taking this one 'classic' or 'pure' instance in Manchester and its environs and uncovering its internal contradictions.

Having in effect already cut himself adrift from his own class, like Marx he was already, by 1845, well down the road to, in the words of the *Communist Manifesto*, 'comprehending theoretically the historical movement as a whole', of grasping that it was with this newly emerging working class that the real future of humanity lay.

As we near the end of the millennium, that future is in greater jeopardy than at any time in history. Capitalism today threatens not simply the working class and the poor people of this planet; it calls into question the very future of the planet itself. Rosa Luxemburg's choice, socialism or barbarism, is not something in prospect but a living reality for millions, a reality far grimmer than those conditions analysed in Manchester by that young arrival from Barmen 150 years ago.

Notes

1 The numbers of long-term unemployed – defined as those out of work for more than a year – have risen dramatically in the industrialised world. Comparing 1979 with 1988, we find that the percentage of long-term unemployed among those out of work rose from 29.2 per cent to 54.8 per cent in the European Union as a whole; in the United States the figure went up from 4.2 per cent to 7.4 per cent, while in the case of Japan the rise was from 16.5 per cent to 20.6 per cent.
2 *LCW* 29, p. 309.
3 See especially his 'Outlines of a Critique of Political Economy' (3: 418–44) later described by Marx as a 'brilliant sketch on the criticism of the economic categories'.
4 *LCW* 2, p. 23.

1. Engels and the Condition of the Working Class Today

Doria Pilling

Does poverty still exist today?

THERE ARE SOME who would deny that poverty still exists in Britain today. It is undoubtedly true that living standards for most workers, employed or unemployed, were incomparably worse in 1844, when Engels wrote *The Condition of the Working Class in England*. The following is one of the many passages – and by no means the most horrific – on the slum areas in which workers lived:

> Every great city has one or more slums, where the working-class is crowded together. True, poverty often dwells in hidden alleys close to the palaces of the rich; but, in general, a separate territory has been assigned to it, where, removed from the sight of the happier classes, it may struggle along as it can. These slums are pretty equally arranged in all the great towns in England, the worst houses in the worst quarters of the towns; usually one or two-storied cottages in long rows, perhaps with cellars used as dwellings, almost all irregularly built. These houses of three or four rooms and a kitchen form, throughout England, some parts of London excepted, the general dwellings of the working class. The streets are generally unpaved, rough, dirty, filled with vegetable and animal refuse, without sewers or gutters, but supplied with foul, stagnant pools instead. Moreover, ventilation is impeded by the bad, confused method of building of the whole quarter, and since many human beings live here crowded into a small space, the atmosphere that prevails in these working men's quarters may readily be imagined. Further, the streets serve as drying grounds in fine weather; lines are stretched across from house to house, and hung with wet clothing. (4: 331)

Here Engels describes workers' clothing:

> The whole clothing of the working class, even assuming it to be
> in good condition, is little adapted to the climate, the damp air of
> England with its sudden changes of temperature, more calculated
> than any other to give rise to colds, obliges almost the whole of
> the middle-class to wear flannel next to the skin, about the body
> and flannel scarves and shirts are in almost universal use. Not
> only is the working class deprived of this precaution, it is scarcely
> ever in a position to use a thread of woollen clothing; and the
> heavy cotton goods, though thicker, stiffer, and heavier than
> woollen clothes, afford much less protection against cold and wet,
> remain damp much longer because of their thickness and the
> nature of the stuff, and have nothing of the compact density of
> fulled woollen cloths. (4: 367)

And their food:

> As with clothing so with food. The workers get what is too bad
> for the property-holding class. In the great towns of England
> everything may be had of the best, but it costs money, and the
> workman, who must keep house on a couple of pence, cannot
> afford much expense. Moreover he usually receives his wages on
> Saturday evening, for, although a beginning has been made in the
> payment of wages on Friday, this excellent arrangement is by no
> means universal; and so he comes to market at five or even seven
> o'clock, while the buyers of the middle-class have had the first
> choice during the morning, when the market teems with the best
> of everything. But when the workers reach it, the best has van-
> ished, and, if it was still there, they would probably not be able
> to buy it. The potatoes which the workers buy are usually poor,
> the vegetables wilted, the cheese old and of poor quality, the
> bacon rancid, the meat lean, tough, taken from old, often diseased
> cattle, or such as have died a natural death, and not fresh even
> then, often half decayed. (4: 368)

It is probably true that no council estate, however dilapidated,
vandalised or crime-ridden, is as bad to live in as the slums
described by Engels. And no one need starve because social security
is available (except for 16–17-year-olds not living at home). People
may go hungry sometimes, life may be dreary, but no one (except
perhaps a few people living on the streets) in Britain is living in
conditions comparable to those in Engels's time. So is it really
accurate to describe those living in the lowest income groups today
as living in poverty?

The idea of measuring poverty in relation to an absolute standard, based on people's minimum needs – of food, clothing and shelter – for survival, has its attractions. This is what Seebohm Rowntree tried to do in 1899, in his study of poverty in York, when those with incomes below the level required to 'obtain the necessaries for the maintenance of merely physical efficiency' were regarded as living in poverty.[1] However, this view has its difficulties. Peter Townsend in his work[2] has campaigned forcefully against it, and his view that poverty has to be defined relatively, in relation to circumstances in society, is generally accepted now. This is not just by campaigning pressure groups like the Child Poverty Action Group, but by such an 'establishment' group, as the members of the Joseph Rowntree Foundation Inquiry Group into Income and Wealth.[3]

How needs can be satisfied is not in itself an absolute, regardless of time and place, but depends on the circumstances of society. It is also argued that poverty is not just about staying alive in a particular society, but being able to participate in its 'normal' activities.[4] The Rowntree Inquiry Group expresses this very well:

> Minimum acceptable living standards are not absolute, but relate to the standards of society as a whole. What might have been an acceptable income twenty, or even ten, years ago is not today. This is not just because society's standards change as it becomes wealthier, but also because life on a fixed real income becomes harder as other people's consumption patterns change with affluence: local shops disappear as the majority use cars; choices of heating fuels become more restricted and expensive; ensuring that children do not feel excluded from the mainstream becomes more expensive as the rising incomes of the majority of parents are reflected in the possessions and consumption of their children. *The falling relative incomes of the poorest are therefore a concern, whether or not those incomes reach or exceed a particular absolute standard of some years ago.* (original emphasis)[5]

It seems quite likely that Engels would have had a similar view. There are several passages in *The Condition* that suggest he had the beginnings of a relative view of needs. For example:

> ... no worker will work for less than he needs to subsist. If he must starve he will prefer to starve in idleness rather than toil. True, this limit is relative; one needs more than another; one is accustomed to more comfort than another; the Englishman who is still somewhat civilised, needs more than the Irishman who goes in rags, eats potatoes and lives in a pigsty (4: 376–7)

Did Engels give a reliable picture of conditions in Britain in 1844?

ENGELS HAS BEEN accused of everything from taking 'too gloomy' an interpretation of the conditions of the British working class in 1844 (criticism of V. A. Huber, 1845, and B. Hildebrand) to handling his material in a way which 'falls below generally accepted standards of scholarship'(Chaloner and Henderson, 1958).[6] Hobsbawm,[7] on the other hand, has defended his account vigorously.

The first point to make is that most of the dire descriptions in *The Condition of the Working Class in England* are not those of Engels himself but are taken from contemporary reports. Engels used a vast amount of material. On a very rough count he used over 30 reports and articles, a number of the latter from the *Journal of the Statistical Society of London*, over 25 official documents, including those of various Commissions of Enquiry (e.g. into Children's Employment, 1842 and 1843; into Sanitary Conditions of the Labouring Population, 1842) and reports of Hansard's Parliamentary Debates (1843 and 1844), plus almost 60 newspaper articles. It is true that the majority (30) of the newspaper items were taken from the *Northern Star*, the central organ of the Chartists, but they can hardly be said to be his main source of evidence overall, and he also used the *Manchester Guardian* (10 items) and *The Times* (8 items) quite extensively.[8] Engels himself says in the Preface to the German Edition:

> Whenever I lacked official documents for describing the condition of the industrial workers, I always preferred to present proof from *Liberal* sources in order to defeat the liberal bourgeoisie by casting their own words in their teeth. I cited Tories or Chartists in my support only when I could confirm their correctness from personal observation or was convinced of the truthfulness of the facts quoted because of the personal or literary reputation of the authorities I referred to. (4: 304)

He also says that he may have made some minor mistakes:

> I know equally well that here and there I may be proved wrong in some particular of no importance, something that in view of the comprehensive nature of the subject, and its far-reaching assumptions, even an Englishman might be unable to avoid; so much the more since even in England there exists as yet not a single piece of writing which, like mine, takes up *all* the workers. But without a moment's hesitation I challenge the English bourgeoisie to prove

that even in a single instance of any consequence for the exposition of my point of view as a whole I have been guilty of any inaccuracy, and to prove it by data as authentic as mine. (4: 303)

Hobsbawm,[9] taking up Chaloner and Henderson's (1958) criticism of Engels, does not dispute the fact that he made numerous minor errors (such as, Engels wrote '16' when the source said '17'), but says that in only a number 'that can be counted on the fingers of two hands' has he been accused of giving a 'wrong or misleading impression of the facts', and challenges the two said to be the most blatant examples of Engels's 'cheating'. He also gives examples of passages where attempts have been made to discredit Engels by saying that the sources themselves use selective material because they were compiled by reformers (or revolutionaries), or that Engels provides insufficient supporting evidence for what he says. And he refutes the proposition that Engels saw the English scene in a particularly gloomy light because he was in the midst of a quarrel with his father, a Rhineland businessman.

It should also be noted that Engels did not say that all workers lived in equally appalling conditions. He describes three particularly horrendous cases, reported in *The Times* and *The Northern Star* – in one, for example, two boys were brought before the magistrate because 'being in a starving condition, they had stolen and immediately devoured a half-cooked calf's foot from a shop', and the magistrate, investigating the case further, found that the mother was a widow, living in a little back room with six childen, and scarcely any furniture, with rags for a bed, as she had been forced to sell her bed to buy food. But he then goes on to say:

I am far from asserting that *all* London working-people live in such want as the foregoing three families. I know very well that ten are somewhat better off, where one is so totally downtrodden under foot by society, but I assert that thousands of industrious and worthy people – far worthier and more to be respected than all the rich of London – do find themselves in conditions unworthy of human beings; and that every proletarian, everyone, without exception, is exposed to a similar fate without any fault of his own and in spite of every possible effort. (4: 335)

Discussing food, he describes differences according to wages:

The habitual food of the individual working-man naturally varies according to his wages. the better-paid workers, especially those in families where every member is able to earn something, have good food as long as this state of things last; meat daily and bacon and cheese for supper. Where wages are less, meat is used only two or three times a week, and the proportion of bread and potatoes increases. Descending gradually, we find the animal food reduced to a small piece of bacon cut up with the potatoes, until on the lowest round of the ladder, among the Irish, potatoes form the sole food. As an accompaniment, weak tea, with perhaps a little sugar, milk or spirits is universally drunk ... But all this presupposes that the workman has work. When he has none, he is wholly at the mercy of accident, and eats what is given him, what he can beg or steal. And if he gets nothing, he simply starves, as we have seen. (4: 372)

Summing up, he says:

Thus the working-class of the great cities offers a graduated scale of the conditions of life, in the best of cases a temporarily endurable existence for hard work and good wages, good and endurable that is from the worker's standpoint; in the worst cases, bitter want, reaching even homelessness and death by starvation. The average is much nearer the worst case than the best. (4: 373)

It would perhaps to be true to say that it is difficult to gauge the shades of poverty in the book, that going from one picture of dire conditions to another said to be even more dire, it is difficult to comprehend the difference. But these faults can be attributed to the author's inexperience, and outrage at what he saw, rather than a biased interpretation. It is instructive here to look at another account of the conditions of the working class in Britain.

In October 1849 a London newspaper, the *Morning Chronicle*, set out to survey the condition of the labouring classes in England and Wales.[10] The country was divided into six regions. The account given here will have to be confined to that of the Manufacturing Districts, which included the cotton industry in Lancashire and Manchester, and which were investigated by a 'high-grade' journalist, Angus Bethune Reach. At the time of his visit, a few years after Engels wrote his book, Manchester was 'neither in the depths of an economic depression ... nor was it experiencing any marked prosperity, and it thus provided an opportunity to discover working class life in a period of normality'.[11] This is what Reach says about the dwellings of the Manchester cotton-working population:

It is not, however, easy to generalise about the subject. The streets of some districts are very far superior to those of others, although the inhabitants of all belong very much to the same class, and the rents paid are tolerably uniform. The old districts are, as might be expected, invariably the worst. They contain the largest proportion of cellar dwellings, of close filthy courts, of undrained lanes, and of rows of houses built back to back, without any provision for ventilation, and with very little for cleanliness. Still a tolerably extensive inspection of the worst localities of Manchester has not revealed to me alleys so utterly squalid and miserable as many I could name in London; and certainly the filthiest court I have penetrated is decency itself compared to the typhus-smelling wynds and closes into which I have adventured in Glasgow. In the older parts of the Borough of Manchester itself, along the great thoroughfare called the Oldham-road, and in the Ancoats district – the latter entirely an operative colony – are situated some of the most squalid-looking streets, inhabited by swarms of the most squalid-looking people which I have seen. Outlying portions of the Borough of Salford are also very miserable, full of streets unpaved, undrained, strewn with offal and refuse, and pierced with airless cul-de-sacs, rendered still more noisome by the quantities of ill-coloured clothes hung to dry from window to window.[12]

The more modern township of Chorlton is, he says, much better, and Hulme, a new district, is the best of all. Even here there were problems with the drains:

Most of the streets were provided with regular drains and gratings. In the case of new streets, I believe that the corporation insists upon these necessary appendages being completed within two years after the completion of the street (it would be as well one would think to make the whole business simultaneous); but the drains in question as I am informed, only carry away the surface water and slops flung into the gutter in the central back passage, all sorts of foul refuse having to be removed by manual labour.

The construction of water-closets is yet a desideratum, even in the best class of operatives' houses; while in the old districts the accommodation in this respect is deficient in the extreme. This is a matter which, in discussing seriously and earnestly the social condition of the people, it would be weak and foolish to shirk. There will be little female virtue where, in the nature of things, there can be little delicacy or decent reserve. In town and in the country, in low lodging houses, and in squalid clusters of agricultural cottages, the evil is the same. The sexes are at all times and all hours huddled together, simply from want of room and accommodation to bestow them separately ...[13]

Nevertheless he was quite optimistic about the future:

Upon the whole then, I am inclined to look hopefully upon the condition of the dwellings of the operative of Manchester. At all events there is an evident disposition to improvement. The corporation are rigid in enforcing the observance of the Local Building act; and as Manchester is still rapidly increasing, the proportion of the better-class dwellings is becoming every day greater. I believe, too, that a very powerful stimulus has been given to increased neatness at home by the additional evening leisure time which the Ten Hours Bill has ensured to the women. 'I have time now to clean my house, and I do it too, every evening' is a phrase I have heard repeated a hundred times by the teneter and female weavers. 'Before, I was so tired that I could do nothing but just eat my supper and go to bed', they generally added. I fear indeed that anything like a thorough reform of that great portion of operative Manchester – built upon a bad plan, or rather no plan at all, save, perhaps, that of promising a yearly return of the greatest number of shillings in the pound – is at present out of the question. It is not, however, I know, beyond the powers of the people, if they be sober and industrious, to keep almost clear of the cellar dwellings.[14]

Sometimes Reach's account is rather less cheerful, describing the vagrant lodging houses, the 'more wretched places still' of the Irish in Manchester, who slept 'huddled on the stones, or on masses of rags, shavings and straw, which were littered about. There was nothing like a bedstead in the place', or the young children given narcotics while their mothers laboured in the mill.

Engels, in his Preface (27: 312) to the English edition of *The Condition*, published in 1892, acknowledges that the 'most crying abuses' described in the book have either 'disappeared or been made less conspicuous'. He attributes this to a number of factors:

The revival of trade after the crises of 1847, was the dawn of a new industrial epoch. The repeal of the Corn Laws and the financial reforms subsequent thereon gave to English industry and commerce all the elbow-room they asked for. The discovery of the Californian and Australian gold-fields followed in rapid succession. The colonial markets developed at an increasing pace in their capacity for absorbing English manufacturing goods ... No wonder England's industrial progress was colossal and unparalleled, and such that the status of 1844 now appears to us as comparatively primitive and insignificant. And in proportion as this increase took place, in the same proportion did manufacturing industry become apparently moralised. The competition of manufacturer against manufacturer by means of petty theft upon the workpeople no longer pays ... Thus the Truck system was suppressed, the Ten Hours' Bill [applying to juveniles 13–18 and women] was enacted, and a number of other secondary reforms introduced ... (27: 308)

The repeated epidemics had also impressed upon the bourgeoisie the need of sanitation for their own benefit.

Near the end of the century, the first attempt was made to define and measure poverty. Charles Booth initially carried out a survey in East London, published in the first volume of *Life and Labour of the People in London* in 1889.

> By the word 'poor' I mean to describe those who have a sufficiently regular though bare income, such as 18s to 21s per week for a moderate family, and by 'very poor' those whose means are insufficient for this according to the usual standard of life in this country. My 'poor' may be described as living under a struggle to obtain the necessaries of life and make both ends meet; while the 'very poor' lie in a state of chronic want.[15]

On this basis, he found that 35.2 per cent of people in East London were living in poverty, a much higher proportion than he had expected.[16] That this was not exceptional was confirmed in the results for the whole of London, published in volume II in 1891. The proportion of 'poor' was found to be 22.3 per cent, of 'very poor', 7.5 per cent, and of the 'lowest class' (occasional labourers, loafers and semi-criminals), 0.9 per cent, making 30.7 per cent in all living in poverty.[17] Poverty was still very extensive near the end of the century, although Britain had, in Engels's words, outgrown the 'juvenile state of capitalist exploitation'.

In his address to the Working Men, which accompanied the 1845 edition of the book, Engels says that his aim was to compile, which no one else had yet done: '... from those rotting blue-books, a single readable book from which everyone might easily get some information on the condition of the great majority of "free-born Britons"' (4: 298). This he undoubtedly accomplished.

'Rediscovering' poverty in Britain

POST-WAR ECONOMIC prosperity and the welfare state were widely seen as eliminating most of the poverty in Britain.[18]

> The 1950s and 1960s were years of such relative affluence that poverty – except presumably by the poor themselves – was almost entirely forgotten. This meant that the public, no doubt encouraged by the mood of the times reflected in Macmillan's 1957 slogan 'You've never had it so good' increasingly felt that most deprivation and disadvantage had been left behind.[19]

But, as Brown and Madge[20] point out, poverty was 'rediscovered' in the 1960s following the publication of several studies, culminating in the influential monograph of Brian Abel-Smith and Peter Townsend.[21] Brown and Madge, writing in the early 1980s, were themselves summing up a research programme lasting almost a decade into the 'cycle of deprivation', a programme which, as they explain, underwent an interesting evolution.

In 1972, Sir Keith Joseph, then Secretary of State for Social Services, made a speech in which he expressed concern about the persistence of poverty and deprivation, despite economic growth and the improvement in the social services. He suggested that there was a 'cycle of transmitted deprivation' problems being transmitted from generation to generation through the family. The initial literature review[22] and research programme that developed changed the emphasis of the enquiry, with a wide range of definitions of deprivation in the various studies, and the investigation of many different possible causal factors. Brown and Madge explain:

> The whole scope of the programme has altered and with it the bias of explanation and indeed of implication. The initial focus was on a minority of severely and multiply deprived families whose various problems in achieving material well-being and emotional and social adjustment appeared to be perpetuated across the generations by their processes of child-rearing. Concentration on such families in small numbers tends inevitably to lead to explanations of their problems in terms of individual pathology, deviant patterns of parenting and maladaptive sub-cultures. By contrast, the wider concern with the level and extent of single derivations within society, tends to lead to explanations in terms of the class structure and the interplay of broad social and economic forces.[23]

In their report Brown and Madge found that – despite striking advances in the standard of living since the end of the Second World War – poverty and deprivation were extensive, not minority problems. At least ten million people were suffering from poverty, four million of them being in families with children. Poverty might be *relative* to the general prosperity, but nevertheless it caused real suffering and had real detrimental consequences.

Engels's picture of the inequalities in society begins to look increasingly more relevant as the twentieth century moves towards its close, though the horrific picture he paints of the conditions of life for the working class in 1844 has fortunately not reappeared for most of those living in poverty in Britain today. It is also clear that the question posed in *The Condition* as to whether the behaviour and attitudes of the poor, and to some extent poverty itself, are caused by 'individual' or 'cultural' factors or by the social conditions under which people live is still very much on the agenda.

The increase of poverty in Britain

IN THE 1990s poverty in Britain is something that no longer has to be 'discovered' or 'uncovered'. A report, published early in 1995, summarising the findings of research projects on income and wealth, funded by the Joseph Rowntree Foundation, stated:

> *One of our particular concerns is with the living standards and life opportunities of the poorest. In many areas of the UK these are unacceptably low in a society as rich as ours.* Evidence from the surveys shows that a substantial proportion of the population is unable to afford the goods which the majority of the population regards as basic necessities, and that many of those dependent on state benefits – particularly for long periods – are unable to make ends meet, or are doing so by accumulating ever higher levels of debt and arrears. If such low incomes were a temporary phenomenon, there might be less cause for concern, but there is disturbing evidence that lengths of time with low incomes, for instance because of lack of work, are becoming longer. (original emphasis)[24]

This report, widely publicised in the media, can hardly be accused of putting an extreme left-wing interpretation on the findings. It was compiled by a Group including Howard Davies, then Director General of the Confederation of British Industry (Deputy Chairman of the Group), Michael Bett, Deputy Chairman of British Telecom, Robin Wendt, Chief Executive of the Association of County Councils, John Williams, Features Editor of the *Financial Times*, and John Monks, General Secretary of the Trades Union Congress.

One of the concerns of the Rowntree Inquiry Group was the sharp rise in income inequality in the 1980s, which became dramatic in the second half of the decade. The share (after the deduction of housing costs on the Households Below Average Incomes (HBAI) series) of the richest tenth of the population increased from 21 per cent in 1979 to 27 per cent in 1991/92, while for the poorest tenth it fell from 4 to 2 per cent. This contrasted with the decline in inequality that occurred at least from the late 1940s to 1976/77 (as indicated by the official 'Blue Book' series, which ran from 1949 to 1984/85). The detailed evidence from the research programme and other sources is set out by John Hills in the second volume of the Rowntree Foundation report.[25] It includes a series produced by Goodman and Webb at the Institute of Fiscal Studies,[26] specially commissioned by the Joseph Rowntree Foundation to provide figures, using Family Expenditure Survey data, on the same basis as the HBAI series, (which started in 1979) but going back to 1961.

The Rowntree report disposed of the 'trickle down' theory that the Conservative Government in the Thatcher era had used to justify increasing inequality. This, it was claimed, would encourage faster economic growth, and those with lower incomes would still be better off despite a fall in their share of total income. From 1979 average real disposable income (i.e. allowing for inflation, and after direct taxation) rose sharply, by 36 per cent (after deduction of housing benefit) over a 12–13-year period to 1991/92. Only the top three-tenths of income groups, though, had incomes rising as fast as this, growth reaching 60 per cent for the top tenth. For the bottom tenth, income in real terms actually fell by 17 per cent. This was in complete contrast to the position in the earlier part of the post-war period. From the late 1940s, average income had been rising, and until the late 1970s it had been rising fastest for those in the bottom income groups.

That there has been a dramatic growth of people living in poverty can be seen from other figures. There is no official 'poverty line' in Britain, but income support (formerly supplementary benefit) level is often taken as this. The 'Low Income Families' series gives the numbers at or below this level. In 1979 7.7 million people, 14 per cent of the population, were living at or below this level, but by 1989 the figure had risen to 11.3 million, 20 per cent of the population.[27] Eight million were living *below* income support level. The HBAI series also provides evidence. In 1979, 1.7 million people had incomes below 40 per cent of the average income (allowing for family circumstances and after housing costs), while by 1991/92 the figure had increased nearly five-fold to 7.9 million. Over three (3.2) million of these had incomes below 40 per cent of the 1979 average.[28] If 50 per cent of average income is taken as the threshold (as is favoured by the Child Poverty Action Group[29]), the rise is from 5 million in 1979 to 13.9 million in 1991/92, with 6 million of these below half of the 1979 average. Goodman and Webb,[30] examining the number of people with incomes below 40, 50 or 60 per cent thresholds, and presenting figures before the deduction of housing costs, show relative stability for the poorest group from the mid-1960s to the mid-1990s while, in their words, this group 'exploded' in numbers in the late 1980s and early 1990s.

The Households Below Average Income, and the Low Income Statistics are both derived from the Family Expenditure survey, and do not include people living in institutions, or the homeless. In 1991 420,000 adults and children were accepted as homeless by the local authorities in England.[31] Shelter[32] estimates that the number of 'unofficial homeless' could be as high as 1.7 million, including about 8,000 people sleeping rough. There are a growing proportion of 16–17-year-olds among the homeless. Sixty-three per cent had no income at all. Thirty-six per cent were from black and ethnic minority groups.

The causes of increasing income inequality

A CONSIDERABLE number of factors have contributed to the increase in income inequality in Britain between the late 1970s and the early 1990s – increasing unemployment, greater disparity between the earnings of high and low earners, the growth in couples in which neither is earning, increasing self-employment, increasing income from investments, the declining relative values of benefits, and changes in the taxation system.[33]

In their analyses, Goodman and Webb[34] look at the composition of groups with incomes below various fractions of national average income. Taking the 40 per cent of average income threshold, in 1961 a million pensioners had incomes below this level, but the number fell to almost zero from 1976 to the mid-1980s and then increased again to the million mark. Over this period the number of very poor families with children having incomes below this level almost trebled (from 906,000 to 2.4 million), the number of single people with children increased ten-fold (from 58,000 to 619,000), and the number of single childless people almost trebled (from 354,000 to 976,000).

The fluctuation in the number of pensioners is accounted for by government policy, which was, until 1980, to increase the basic state pension each year in line with movements in prices or earnings, whichever was higher. The stopping of earnings indexation took several years before it left those mainly dependent on state pensions well below the national average income. It has been estimated that the pension would have been £19.35 higher for a single person and £30.65 higher in April 1993 had the old method of uprating still been in force.[35]

The numbers of unemployed increased in the group of those with incomes 40 per cent below national average from the late 1960s, with a sharp rise in the late 1980s, the numbers increasing thirteen-fold over the whole period (from 101,000 to 1.3 million).[36] The big increase in families with children among the poorest in Britain is largely due to the increase in mass unemployment, according to Goodman and Webb. The real value of unemployment benefit has changed little from 1970 to 1993, but it has fallen in relation to national average income throughout this period.[37] Since 1988 it has become more difficult to claim unemployment benefit, because this relies on contributions paid in the two previous years, rather than one, and rules about availability for work, and actively seeking work have become more stringent.[38] Unemployment benefit only lasts for a year, and after this people are forced on to means-tested income support.

20

There has also been a considerable increase in earnings' disparity. Wages for the lowest paid (bottom tenth) of male earners have hardly changed since 1978 and by 1992 were lower in real terms than in 1975. In contrast, wages for the most highly paid (the top tenth), have increased by 50 per cent. Median wages increased by 35 per cent. Before this period, between 1966 and 1977, wages at all levels had grown at the same rate.[39] The gap between high and low male wages is now wider than at any time in the century for which there are records. It has been suggested that the increased dispersion of wages is the result of two factors: an increased demand for workers with high educational qualifications, due to technological developments, which has driven up the wages of skilled workers; and increasing international trade, which has meant that unskilled workers have to compete with workers in countries where wages are much lower.[40] Other suggested reasons are the declining importance of trade unions, and the decline of minimum wage regulation through the wage councils. The lowest paid younger male workers are earning less then their predecessors and trends suggest that there is little chance of their earnings increasing with age. Taking all young workers, 18–20-year-olds earned 61 per cent of the earnings of those aged 21+ in 1979, but only 53 per cent of their earnings in 1991.[41]

In general, the proportion of gross family income contributed by women grew during the 1980s, the exception being in couples where the man was out of work. Between 1975 and 1993 there has been a rise in the proportion of two-adult households both with two earners (from 52 per cent to 61 per cent) and with no earners (from 4 per cent to 11 per cent).[42] Chances of getting back into work for men and women in no-earner couples has decreased, the main factor being the shift towards part-time and temporary work. These opportunities are disproportionately taken by those in working households, while full-time opportunities, the availability of which has fallen by a third since 1975, are disproportionately taken by workless families. It is likely that the disincentives of the benefits system play a part in this. Where a family is living on income support, earnings are deducted pound for pound from benefit, after a small disregard. If a man becomes unemployed, it may not be worthwhile financially for his wife to continue working.[43]

There has also been a considerable increase in self-employment (from 7.3 per cent of the employed in 1979 to 13.5 in 1990).[44] The share of household income contributed by self-employment has not risen so rapidly, suggesting that it often consists of low-income work (though some self-employed are among the highest earners).[45] The Government's Enterprise Allowance scheme has encouraged self-employment amongst people who are unemployed and unable to get other work.

Investment income has also been found to be a major contributor to the growth in income inequality.[46] Discretionary changes (those of the kind announced on Budget day) in the tax system in the 1980s have had an effect as well, cancelling out the automatic effect the progressive tax system should have had in reducing inequality.[47]

Women and poverty

WOMEN ESPECIALLY IN Britain today bear the brunt of poverty. This is nothing new, as several authors have pointed out (see chapters in Glendinning and Millar's book, *Women in Poverty in Britain*).[48] Women have tended to be invisible in official statistics on poverty, because income is measured in terms of tax, family or household units, and not broken down by sex.[49] It has been calculated, though, that there were one-and-a-half times as many women in poverty as men in 1989, making assumptions about the numbers of women who were lone parents, pensioners and so on: 5.1 million women and 3.4 million men were on or below the income support level.[50]

The one group of women who are highly visible are lone mothers, and they are constantly under attack from Conservative politicians (for example, in the speech by Peter Lilley to the Conservative Way Forward Group, on 7 October 1993) for their cost to the country in benefits. There has certainly been a big increase in this group. the number of one-parent families with children rose from 570,000 in 1971 to an estimated 1.4 million in 1992,[51] though, it should be noted, there are still two parents in 79 per cent of families with children. In about 90 per cent of cases in one-parent families it is the mother who is the lone parent, and although most are divorced, separated or widowed, there has been a considerable increase of single, never-married mothers, from 1 percent in 1971 to 7 per cent in 1992. Not much evidence is available yet on the reasons for this,[52] but they do not appear to include the 'ulterior motive' of gaining council housing, as claimed by some Conservative politicians.[53]

What is certain is that the majority of lone parents live in poverty. Seven out of ten lone parents with dependent children – including nine out of ten single mothers – are receiving income support, either because they are not working, or they are earning little enough to be eligible while working fewer than 16 hours a week.[54] (Today's lone parents are at greater risk of living in poverty than those of 20 years ago, when just over a third received supplementary benefit, the predecessor of income support.)[55] Sixty per cent of lone parents in 1992 had gross weekly incomes of less than £150 a week, compared with only 11 per cent of married and cohabiting parents.[56] Unlike the position in two-parent families, employment is no more common among lone parents than it was ten years ago, and it is 20 per cent lower than among married and cohabiting mothers with dependent children. The difference is largely in part-time employment.[57] The difficulty of obtaining good child-care at a reasonable cost, which may be greatest for lone mothers, because they do not have husbands to help and may not be able to afford as much as married mothers, appeared to be an important reason.[58] The provision of publicly funded child-care in Britain is worse than in most other European countries.[59] However, the main reason in a national sample survey of lone mothers appeared to be their 'perceptions of the needs of, and their responsibilities towards, their children'.[60] Lone mothers face an acute dilemma, being blamed by politicians and others for society's ills, including drug abuse and crime, and yet begrudged sufficient support to bring up their children, even though research of many years' standing has shown that economic difficulties are the main problem families in this situation face.[61]

In two-parent families mothers are increasingly returning to work, and returning sooner after their children are born.[62] Sixty-five per cent of women with dependent children were 'economically active' in 1992 (59 per cent employed, 6 per cent unemployed,[63] compared with 49 per cent in 1973). Two-thirds were in part-time jobs. Both parents now work in 60 per cent of families. The main reason is the drastic decline in the earnings of unskilled men. Prior to the 1980s it had been the wives of relatively well-paid men whose employment had increased most rapidly. In the 1980s it was employment of women in lower income families, in the 24–55 age-group (apart from those in the lowest tenth), which increased most.[64] The share contributed by women's earnings to gross family income grew most in families where the men had low or median earnings. Had it not been for women's pay, the rate of poverty among married and cohabiting couples would have been 13.1 per cent rather than 8.1 per cent in 1990/91, 50 per cent higher than it was.

Nevertheless this means that more women were under the pressure of having to carry out dual roles – in the home and at work. Even where they work full-time, chores are still today mainly carried out by women in two-thirds of households.[65] In 78 per cent of households it is mainly the woman who does the washing and ironing, in 63 per cent it is she who mainly does the cleaning, in 60 per cent she gets the evening meal, while men have the main responsibility only for doing household repairs.

In the 1980s there was a shift in Britain to 'precarious' or 'flexible' employment. By 1986 a third of the workforce, 8.1 million, were in this kind of employment, about 5.1 million were part-time workers, 2.7 million were self-employed and 1.6 million were temporary workers.[66] Between 1979 and 1991 there was a loss of nearly two million full-time male jobs. During the same period there was also an increase in part-time employment, but this mainly involved women: 0.7 million part-time jobs for women and 0.25 million for men.[67] Self-employment, which includes homeworking, increased by 1.3 million during this period. In all about 80 per cent of part-time jobs and 60 per cent of temporary jobs are carried out by women.[68] In 1991 4.46 million women were in part-time jobs.[69]

There are several reasons for the shift to this 'precarious' or 'flexible' work.[70] It was partly due to the decline in manufacturing industry, and expansion of service industries, which are more scattered and often have extended opening hours to suit customers. However, much seems to be a way of cost-cutting for employers – transforming fixed costs into variable costs. The regular wage bill and associated costs, like national insurance, pensions contributions, office overheads, are transformed into lower costs only payable for the duration of the contract. It has also been encouraged by privatisation and compulsory competitive tendering, those putting in the lowest tender winning the contract – often meaning that workers are paid less, work fewer hours and lose various benefits like holiday pay, pension rights, and so on. The development of information technology also made its contribution, for example enabling management to keep track of a large and scattered workforce.

Even taking full-time work, women earn considerably less than men. Although women's earnings have risen in relation to those of men (probably not unconnected with the implementation of the Equal Pay Act)[71] their median full-time earnings were still only 73 per cent of those of men in 1994 (compared with 53 per cent in 1968).[72] Women part-time workers do worse. In 1991 women part-time workers were paid only 58 per cent of the gross hourly earnings of full-time male workers, excluding overtime work (£4.40 an hour compared with £7.57 for men).[73] The low pay is partly due to the segregation of men's and women's work, which has allowed a different wage structure to grow up, keeping women's pay low.[74] Women earning below the national insurance level (£58 a week in 1992), around a million, also miss out on benefits such as sick pay, maternity pay, unemployment benefit and pensions.[75] It is estimated that between one and two million people, mainly women, are homeworkers, and that they are often paid exceptionally low rates. A West Yorkshire Homeworking Unit report[76] found an average hourly rate of pay in the 1980s of 82 pence.

Women earn less than men both because they have lower rates of pay and because they work fewer hours. Analysis of men's and women's pay in 1977 – using the 1946 longitudinal study, the National Survey of Health and Development – found an unexplained gap of about 30 per cent, after explanatory variables such as education and employment experience and job characteristics had been taken into account.[77] This gap is suggested as being probably due to sex discrimination. Further analyses investigated the effects of parenthood, finding that this had little effect on men's labour participation or pay but that it had consequences such as lost employment experience, downward mobility and lower pay rates for part-time work, which lowered pay in comparison with that of women contemporaries without children by 15 per cent.

Women's disadvantage in the labour market is directly related to the still prevailing attitude that they should have the main responsibility for looking after others – their children, elderly and sick relatives and their husbands. This penalises them not only in relation to the hours they are able to work and rates of pay, but means that they may lose out on state and occupational benefits. The rules governing eligibility are geared to male patterns of employment and earnings, and women with limited or discontinuous employment may not qualify.[78] The result is that women are more likely to be dependent on mean-tested benefits, and they are also more likely than men to experience poverty in old age.

What it means to be poor in today's Britain

IT IS ALSO mainly women who have the job of eking out the scarce resources to meet the family's needs. That living below the poverty line, whether this is measured by the income support level or that of half the national average income, is insufficient to provide an adequate standard of living by today's standards is shown in a study by the Family Budget Unit at the University of York.[79] They drew up what was considered to be a modest but adequate budget for different family types, drawing on a panel of experts and consumer groups and using expenditure data. Items were included in the budget if they were regarded as necessities in public opinion surveys or they were possessed by more than half of the population. For example, a fridge-freezer, washing machine, microwave, food-mixer and sewing machine were included, but a tumble dryer, shower and electric blankets excluded. One week's annual holiday was included, but a holiday abroad excluded. Income support level met only just above a third of the costs of this budget (34 per cent to 39 per cent for all family types), and the income represented by half the national average family income around half (40 per cent to 59 per cent), with a family consisting of a lone mother and two children doing worst.

This study suggests that poor families not only have to do without modest luxuries but essentials. Two recent studies[80] confirm that income support or low wages are not sufficient to provide a reasonable standard of living in today's Britain. Linda Morris and Jane Ritchie's study[81] was concerned with the living standards of three groups of families with dependent children: those claiming income support because of unemployment or part-time work; those in employment but receiving income-related benefits (i.e. housing benefit, family credit, council tax rebate); and those in employment with median earnings, not eligible for income-related benefits. Those in the income support group were likely to be unskilled workers, with significant unemployment and insecurity in the past, those employed with in-work benefits were fairly similar, while those employed and not eligible for income-related benefits were usually skilled or non-manual workers with a more secure employment history. It was found that only those with income about midway in the median income group had 'a sense of reasonable comfort for all household members'. The analysis distinguished between 'contracted expenditure', that which families are in some way contracted to pay (such as housing costs, utility bills, credit and debt repayments) and 'noncontracted expenditure', the former ranging from about 50 per cent to 80 per cent of net income in all groups. Where 'contracted expenditure' was disproportionately high this was primarily due to credit and debt repayment. In the income support group this was often made up of arrears or credit for large domestic items. These families had a great struggle to make ends meet on their residual income. Almost all of the income support group and about half of the in-work benefits group were said to regularly face competing demands for the purchase of food, children's clothing, and the payment of regular bills.

> At the lowest resource levels there are couples who regularly go without food, have difficulty in clothing children, have to deny them recreational spending, and are severely constrained, and sometimes thrown into further debt, by conventional celebrations.[82]

This was not because of bad management. The researchers say 'the general picture was one of stringent or frugal managing which at the end of the fortnight often failed'.

The second study, by Elaine Kempson, Alex Bryson and Karen Rowlingson of the Policy Studies Institute[83] also has much to say about the management of scanty resources. The sample here also consisted of three groups, this time all low-income families living in inner city areas. One group was on income support, the second was receiving low wages which made them eligible for family credit, and the third had incomes which put them on the margin of eligibility for family credit. Only 18 of the 74 families had no arrears and half owed money to two or more creditors. Debts were most likely to be due to arrears on the poll tax, housing commitments or bills for utilities. Two main strategies were used for budget management, termed by the researchers 'minimising expenditure' and 'bill juggling'. 'Minimising expenditure' meant keeping a very tight control of resources and cutting back severely in an attempt to avoid borrowing or getting behind with bills. 'Bill juggling' was often combined with borrowing to pay bills, rather than severely curtailing expenditure, and usually resulted in multiple arrears. Families did not necessarily adopt a single approach to managing resources but often changed their strategy when their circumstances changed, particularly if they suffered a big drop in income or got into debt. The most important finding was that both strategies carried a heavy cost. Bill jugglers attempted to minimise sacrifices on material well-being and social participation, particularly for the children, but faced disconnections, court appearances and threats of eviction, as well as fears of the children being taken into care. Those who adopted the more socially approved method of minimising expenditure sacrificed social activities and cut back on food. Mothers often went without food to feed the children: 'I don't cut down, as I say with the kids. I try to make sure they get, but like I cook a meal and as long as there's plenty for them, I make do with a piece of toast.'[84] They also cut back on fuel, especially where, which was common, they had pre-payment meters. One said: 'I try to cut down on me electric. Many a Sunday afternoon our electric has gone. We've just waited till Monday.'[85] She had contingency plans, using a camping light and wiring the television up to a car battery when the meter ran out. The families who cut back severely on spending avoided creditors pursuing them, but as the researchers put it: 'it was the relentlessness of their existence that got people down'. Cutting back on food is not exceptional, a National Children's Home study[86] finding that among 345 low income families one in five parents and one in ten children had gone hungry in the past month because they did not have enough money to buy food.

Both the Kempson, Bryson and Rowlingson study and the Morris and Ritchie study found that additional resources were crucial to the families' survival. This might take the form of casual earnings – sometimes undeclared, bringing additional anxieties – pawning and selling possessions, and help from family and friends, who were often little better off than they were. Many families preferred help from those in similar financial circumstances, and they expected to help others when they were able to.

Engels today

WHILE FOR MOST members of the working class, whether employed or unemployed, the conditions of life in Britain in the 1990s bear little resemblance to the appalling conditions of 1844, some of the aspects of capitalist production that are reappearing – unemployment, insecure employment, the decline in employment opportunities for men and rise in those for women – are among those that Engels wrote so graphically about.

Unemployment does not lead to starvation today – although there is evidence of it being linked with ill-health and suicide among men[87] – but the feelings of insecurity described, that it can happen to anyone and that it is no fault of the individual, are relevant in today's world of 'flexible' employment:

> True, it is only individuals who starve, but what security has the working man that it may not be his turn tomorrow? Who assures his employment, who vouches for it, if for any reason or no reason his lord and master discharges him tomorrow, he can struggle along with those dependent upon him, until he may find some one else 'to give him bread'? Who guarantees that willingness to work shall suffice to obtain work, that uprightness, industry, thrift and the rest of the virtues recommended by the bourgeoisie are really his road to happiness? No one. He knows that he has something today, and that it does not depend upon himself whether he shall have something tomorrow. He knows that every breeze that blows, every whim of his employer, every bad turn of trade may hurl him back into the fierce whirlpool from which he has temporarily saved himself, and in which it is hard and often impossible to keep his head above water. He knows that, though he may have the means of living today, it is very uncertain whether he shall tomorrow. (4: 330–1)

Engels's views on the employment of women, however, might well, at least at first sight, win the approval of today's Conservative politicians. Talking about the crowding out of adult males from factories, where he says in 1839 only a quarter of the operatives were adult males, he goes on:

> The employment of women at once breaks up the family; for when the wife spends twelve or thirteen hours every day in the mill, and the husband works the same length of time, what happens to the children? They grow up like wild weeds; they are put out to nurse for a shilling or eighteen pence a week, and how they are treated may be imagined. Hence the accidents to which little children fall victims multiply in the factory districts to a terrible extent. (4: 436)

Later Engels says:

> The children who grow up under such conditions are utterly ruined for later family life, can never feel at home in the family which they

themselves found, because they have always been accustomed to isolation, and they contribute therefore to the already general undermining of the family in the working-class. (4: 437)

Sometimes, he says, the employment of women leads not to the family being wholly dissolved, but to it being turned upside down, with the man's and woman's role being reversed. One of the most poignant passages in the whole of the *The Conditions* is the letter in which a working man relates the situation in which another working-man found an old friend:

And when my poor friend went in, there sat poor Jack near the fire, and what did he, think you. Why he sat and mended his wife's stockings with the bodkin: and as soon as he saw his old friend at the door post, he tried to hide them. But Joe, that is my friend's name, had seen it and said: 'Jack, what the devil art thou doing? Where is the missus. Why is that thy work?' and poor Jack was ashamed and said: 'No, I know that it is not my work, but my poor missus is i' the' factory: she has to leave at half-past five and works till eight at night, and then she is so knocked up that she cannot do aught when she gets home, so I have to do everything for her what I can do, for I have no work, nor had any for more nor three years, and I shall never have any more while I live', and then he wept a big tear. Jack again said: 'There is work enough for women folks and childer hereabouts, but none for men: thou mayest sooner find a hundred pound on the road than work for men – but I should never have believed that either thou or anyone else would have seen me mending my wife's stockings, for it is bad work. But she can hardly stand on her feet. I am afraid she will be laid up, and then I don't know what is to become of us, for it's a good bit that she has been the man in the house and I the woman ...' and Jack began to cry again, and he wished he had never been married, and that he had never been born ... (4: 438)

Such sentiments have by no means died out today, and men do still feel that they should be the main breadwinner. The phenomenon of the 'no-earner' family is causing much debate, though there is a difference of views as to whether the reason for neither partner working when the man is unemployed is due to traditional views[88] or social security disincentives.[89]

Engels's immediate reaction to the letter quoted above might suggest that he was simply a man of his time, sharing these traditional views:

Can anyone imagine a more insane state of things than that described in this letter? And yet this condition, which unsexes the man and takes from the woman all womanliness, without being able to bestow on the man true womanliness, or the woman true manliness – this condition which degrades, in the most shameful way, both sexes, and, through them, Humanity, is the last result of our much-praised civilisation, the final achievement of all the efforts and struggles of hundreds of generations to improve their own situation and that of posterity. (4: 439)

As the passage continues, a rather different light is thrown on Engels's views:

We must either despair of mankind, and its aims and efforts, when we see all our labour and toil result in such a mockery, or we must admit that human society has hitherto sought salvation in a false direction; we must admit that so total a reversal of the position of the sexes can have only come to pass because the sexes have been placed in a false position from the beginning. If the reign of wife over the husband, as inevitably brought about by the factory system, is inhuman, the pristine rule of the husband over the wife must have been inhuman too. If the wife can now base her supremacy upon the fact that she supplies the greater part, nay, the whole of the common possession, the necessary inference is that this community of possession is no true and rational one, since one member of the family boasts offensively of contributing the greater share. If the family of our present society is thus being dissolved, this dissolution shows that, at bottom, the binding tie of this family was not family affection, but private interest lurking under the cloak of a pretended community of possession. (4: 439)

Indeed, this position, in 1844, querying the domination of man over woman, seems very perceptive, when over 140 years later it can still be argued in the chapter introducing a book on *Women and Poverty in Britain*:

However, this book is more than simply a description of the extent of poverty among women in Britain today. It also explores the causes of that poverty. It locates those causes firmly in a sexual division of labour which marginalises women's involvement in the labour market, while at the same time assigning little or no value to their caring and domestic work within the family. *Central to this division of labour is a widespread assumption that women are – and should be – financially dependent on men.* ... Women's own economic circumstances are obscured under assumptions about their dependence on men. The focus of both research and policy is therefore generally on the ability of men to provide, through waged labour or welfare, for women and other dependants. We shall argue that, as a consequence, women experience considerable economic disadvantage in the labour market and in the private and public systems of welfare, both of which are fashioned to and dependent on male-oriented patterns of employment. (emphasis added)[90]

The 'underclass' today and in Engels's time

THE 'UNDERCLASS' is today a fashionable term, used extensively in the media. Despite this, despite intense academic debate over its meaning,[91] despite a long history of similar concepts, it is an imprecise concept. However, as Dean and Taylor-Gooby[92] put it, it is so popular because it has managed to '"capture" a range of concerns'. Take this definition, from the *New York Times* in 1987:

> Social scientists have focused new energies on an 'underclass' of Americans who live in near total isolation from mainstream society, and scholars are trying to learn more about the inner-city areas where not working is the norm, crime is commonplace and welfare is a way of life.[93]

Like most definitions of the underclass, it combines concerns about delinquency, dependency and unemployment (and, in the United States, at least, about race and ghettos). Predominantly, the concept of the underclass is favoured by those on the right of the political spectrum, who define it by the behaviour of certain groups in society. The chief proponent of the idea in the United States is the ultra-conservative Charles Murray. In an article in the *Sunday Times* (26 November 1989) he said:

> When I use the term 'underclass' I am indeed focusing on a certain type of poor person, defined not by his condition – e.g. long-term unemployed – but by his deplorable behaviour in response to that condition – e.g. unwilling to take the jobs that are available to him.

Murray has two major concerns: the rising rate of never-married black mothers, and the non-participation of young black men in the labour market. He blames both on the welfare system, which enables a couple to remain unmarried and live off the woman's welfare claim. There is a wide range of evidence against this view.[94] The most puzzling part about Murray's argument is that the young unemployed do not themselves have a claim to welfare, the main welfare programmes being linked to having dependent children, so there seems little incentive for young black males to deliberately remain out of the labour market.[95]

Others in the United States have had a 'structural' definition of the underclass. Douglas Glasgow,[96] for example, saw the underclass as: 'a permanently entrapped population of poor persons, unused and unwanted, accumulated in various parts of the country'. Blacks were disproportionately represented among the group. Difficulties in obtaining employment, racism, and rejection from mainstream institutions, especially schools, appeared to be the main factors forming an underclass.

It was in this kind of way that the term was used by Frank Field, a Labour MP who has long campaigned against poverty.[97] He saw government policies and unemployment trends as making it increasingly difficult for people to escape poverty. Members of the underclass, in his view, consisted of a heterogeneous grouping of the long-term unemployed, lone parents and elderly people dependent solely on state benefits.

Whether it is helpful to use the term in this way is debatable. One of the studies in the 'cycle of deprivation' research programme, mentioned earlier in the chapter,[98] investigating families with multiple social disadvantages in the National Child Development Study, found considerable turnover over time: only a third of the children and their families classified as multiply disadvantaged at 11 were still in this category at 16; and half of those multiply disadvantaged at 16 had not been so at 11.[99] My own study, following on from this, indicated considerable discontinuity as well as the continuity of social disadvantage (Pilling, 1990).[100] Sometimes an accumulation of problems, or the effects of problems, prevented people from taking opportunities, but most took those offered. Other studies also suggest that people who are long-term unemployed or on benefits[101] have the same attitudes as the rest of society. Using the term 'underclass' might prompt investigation into whether it is now more difficult to get out of poverty than in the past. However, the connotations of individual or cultural blame are more likely to obscure the structural causes of poverty.

From *The Condition*, there is little doubt that Engels has a 'structural explanation' for workers who are thrown into poverty, and for their behaviour. He clearly sees the poor not as separated from the rest of the working class, but being in a situation to which anyone might be thrown by misfortune:

... And this series does not fall into fixed classes so that one can say, this fraction of the working class is well off, has always been so, and remains so. If that is the case here and there, if single branches of work have in general an advantage over others, yet the condition of the workers in each branch is subject to such great fluctuations that a single working-man be so placed as to pass through the whole range from comparative comfort to the extremest need, even to death by starvation, while almost every English working-man can tell a tale of marked changes of fortune. (4: 374)

It is the needs of production, not the behaviour of individuals, which results in workers being unemployed. And when they are, their behaviour is determined by their situation:

So it goes on perpetually – prosperity, crisis, prosperity, crisis, and this perennial round in which English industry moves is, as has been observed before usually completed in six years.
From this it is clear that the English manufacture must have at all times, save the brief periods of highest prosperity, an unemployed reserve army of workers, in order to be able to produce the masses of good required by the market in the liveliest months ...
This reserve army, which embraces an immense multitude during the crisis and a large number during the period which may be regarded as average between the highest prosperity and the crisis, is the 'surplus' population of England, which keeps body and souls together by begging, stealing, street-sweeping, collecting manure, pushing hand-carts, driving donkeys, peddling or performing occasional small jobs. In every great town a multitude of such people may be found. (4: 383–4)

Even in regard to the Irish, whom Engels sometimes does seem to be saying have a 'culture of poverty', though certainly not one which makes them withdraw from the labour market, he sees social conditions as the main determinant of behaviour:

The temptation is great, he cannot resist it, and so when he gets his money he gets rid of it down his throat. What else should he do? How can society blame him, when it places him in a position in which he almost of necessity becomes a drunkard, when it leaves him to himself, to his savagery? (4: 391–2)

Engels does see the situation of the working class as giving it different values, behaviour and attitudes from the bourgeoisie:

In view of all this, it is not surprising that the working-class has gradually become a race wholly apart from the English bourgeoisie. The bourgeoisie has more in common with every other nation of the earth than the workers in whose midst he lives. The workers speak other dialects, have other thoughts and ideals, other customs and moral principles, a different religion, and other politics than the bourgeoisie. (4: 420)

However, the working-class is far from being trapped in a sub-culture. On the contrary the emancipation of all humanity is its responsibility.

Communism stands in principle above the breach between the bourgeoisie and proletariat, recognises only its historic significance for the present, but not its justification for the future: wishes indeed to bridge over this chasm, to do away with all class antagonisms. Hence it recognises as justified, so long as the struggle exists, the exasperation of the proletariat towards its oppressors as a necessary, as the most important lever for the labour movement just beginning; but it goes beyond this exasperation, because Communism is a question of humanity and not of the workers alone. Besides it does not occur to any Communist to wish to revenge himself upon individuals or believe that, in general, the single bourgeois can act otherwise, under existing circumstances, than he does act. (4: 581–2)

Notes

1 See P. Keating (ed.), *Into Unknown England: 1866–1913. Selections from the Social Explorers*, Manchester University Press, 1976, pp. 189–90.
2 See, for example, P. Townsend, *Poverty in the United Kingdom: A Survey of Household and Living Standards*, Allen Lane and Penguin Press, 1979; *The International Analysis of Poverty*, Harvester Wheatsheaf, 1993.
3 This group included, for example, Howard Davis, then Director General of the Confederation of British Industry.
4 See Townsend, *Poverty in the United Kingdom*.
5 P. Barclay, *Joseph Rowntree Foundation Inquiry into Income and Wealth*, vol. 1, Joseph Rowntree Foundation, 1995, p. 33.
6 Criticisms mentioned in E. J. Hobsbawm. Introduction to F. Engels, *The Condition of the Working Class in England*, Granada, 1975.
7 Ibid., and E. J. Hobsbawm, *Labouring Men*, Weidenfeld and Nicolson, 1964, p. 105.
8 Source: Index of Quoted and Mentioned Literature. (4: 741–61)
9 Hobsbawm, *Labouring Men*.
10 I. J. Ginswick, *Labour and the Poor in England and Wales 1849–1851*, vol. 1, Lancashire, Cheshire, Yorkshire, Frank Cass, 1983.
11 Ibid.
12 Ibid., p. 18.
13 Ibid., p. 20.
14 Ibid., p. 26.

15 See Keating (ed.), *Into Unknown England*, pp. 112–40.

16 Ibid., p. 25.

17 Ibid., p. 134.

18 J. Scott, *Poverty and Wealth: Citizenship, Deprivation and Privilege*, Longman, 1994.

19 M. Brown and N. Madge, *Despite the Welfare State*, Heinemann, 1982, p. 13.

20 Ibid.

21 B. Abel-Smith and P. Townsend, *The Poor and the Poorest*, Occasional Papers on Social Administration, no. 17, G. Bell and Sons Ltd, 1965.

22 M. Rutter and N. Madge, *Cycles of Disadvantage*, Heinemann, 1976.

23 Brown and Madge, *Despite the Welfare State*, p. 3

24 Barclay, *Joseph Rowntree*, vol. 1, p. 33.

25 J. Hills, *Joseph Rowntree Foundation Inquiry into Income and Wealth*, vol. 2, Joseph Rowntree Foundation. The analysis of HBAI series data was carried out by S. Jenkins, *Winners and Losers: A Portrait of the UK Income Distribution During the 1980s*, University College Swansea, 1994. Despite its name the data on which the HBAI series is based covers all income groups.

26 A. Goodman and S. Webb, *For Richer, For Poorer, the Changing Distribution of Income in the United Kingdom, 1961–1991*, Institute for Fiscal Studies, 1994.

27 C. Oppenheim, *Poverty: The Facts*, CPAG, 1993.

28 Hills, *Joseph Rowntree*, vol. 2.

29 Oppenheim, *Poverty: The Facts*.

30 Goodman and Webb, *For Richer, For Poorer*.

31 Shelter, 1992, cited by Oppenheim, *Poverty: The Facts*.

32 Ibid.

33 Goodman and Webb, *For Richer, For Poorer*; Hills, *Joseph Rowntree*, vol. 2.

34 Ibid.

35 Oppenheim, *Poverty: The Facts*.

36 Goodman and Webb, *For Richer, For Poorer*.

37 Hills, *Joseph Rowntree*, vol. 2.

38 Oppenheim, *Poverty: The Facts*.

39 Gosling, Machin and Meghir, 1994, cited by Hills, *Joseph Rowntree*, vol. 2.

40 Hills, *Joseph Rowntree*, vol. 2.

41 Low Pay Unit, *Poor Britain: Poverty and Inequality and Low Pay in the Nineties*, Low Pay Unit, 1992.

42 P. Gregg and J. Wadsworth, *More Work in Fewer Households*, Social Policy Findings 61, Joseph Rowntree Foundation, 1994.

43 Oppenheim, *Poverty: The Facts*.

44 Meager, Court and Moralee, 1994, cited by Hills, *Joseph Rowntree*, vol. 2.

45 Goodman and Webb, *For Richer, For Poorer*.

46 Ibid.; Jenkins cited by Hills, *Joseph Rowntree*, vol. 2.

47 Johnson and Webb, 1992, and Redmond and Sutherland, in press, both cited by Hills, ibid.

48 C. Glendinning and J. Millar (eds) *Women and Poverty in Britain*, Harvester Wheatsheaf, 1987.
49 J. Millar and C. Glendinning, 'Invisible Women, Invisible Poverty', in ibid.; Oppenheim, *Poverty: The Facts.*
50 Oppenheim, ibid.
51 D. Utting, *Family and Parenthood: Supporting Families, Preventing Breakdown*, Joseph Rowntree Foundation, 1995.
52 Ibid.
53 Phoenix, 1991, cited in ibid.
54 Utting, *Family and Parenthood.*
55 Bradshaw and Millar, 1991, cited in ibid.
56 General Household Survey, cited in ibid.
57 General Household Survey, cited by V. Kumar, *Poverty and Inequality in the UK: The Effects on the Children*, National Children's Bureau, 1993.
58 Kumar, ibid.
59 Oppenheim, *Poverty: The Facts.*
60 Bradshaw and Millar, 1991, cited by Kumar, *Poverty and Inequality.*
61 E. Ferri, *Growing Up in a One-Parent Family*, NFER, 1976.
62 Utting, *Family and Parenthood.*
63 General Household Survey, cited in ibid.
64 S. Harkness, S. Machin and J. Waldfogel, *Women's Pay and Family Income Inequality*, Social Policy Findings 60, Joseph Rowntree Foundation, 1994.
65 British Social Attitudes, 1992, cited by Utting, *Family and Parenthood.*
66 U. Huws, J. Hurstfield and R. Holtmaat, *What Price Flexibility: The Casualisation of Women's Employment*, Low Pay Unit, 1989.
67 Working Brief, 28.11.91, cited by Kumar, *Poverty and Inequality.*
68 Kumar, ibid.
69 Oppenheim, *Poverty: The Facts.*
70 Huws, Hurstfield and Holtmaat, *What Price Flexibility.*
71 H. Joshi, 'The Changing Form of Women's Dependency', in H. Joshi (ed.), *The Changing Population of Britain*, Blackwell.
72 Hills, *Joseph Rowntree*, vol. 2.
73 New Earnings Survey 1991, cited by Low Pay Unit, *Poor Britain.*
74 Joshi, 'The Changing Form of Women's Dependency'; S. Lonsdale, 'Patterns of Paid Work', in Glendinning and Millar, (eds), *Women and Poverty in Britain.*
75 Low Pay Unit, *Poor Britain.*
76 Cited in ibid.
77 Joshi, 'The Changing Form of Women's Dependency'.
78 Millar and Glendinning, 'Invisible Women, Invisible Poverty'.
79 Bradshaw, Hicks and Palmer, 1992, cited by Oppenheim, *Poverty: The Facts.*
80 E. Kempson, A. Bryson and K. Rowlingson, *Hard Times: How Poor Families Make Ends Meet.* Policy Studies Institute, 1994; L. Morris and J. Ritchie, *Income Maintenance and Living Standards*, Social Policy Findings 65, Joseph Rowntree Foundation, 1994.

81 Morris and Ritchie, ibid.
82 Morris and Ritchie, ibid, p. 3.
83 Kempson, Bryson and Rowlingson, *Hard Times*.
84 Ibid., p. 283
85 Ibid.
86 1991, cited by Oppenheim, *Poverty: The Facts*, p. 75.
87 For example, R. Smith, 'Unemployment: Here We Go Again', *British Medical Journal*, vol. 302, 16 March 1991; and T. Delamothe, 'Poor Britain, Losing Out', *British Medical Journal*, vol. 305, 1 August 1992.
88 For example, Kempson, Bryson and Rowlingson, *Hard Times*.
89 For example, Gregg and Wadsworth, *More Work*.
90 Millar and Glendinning, 'Invisible Women, Invisible Poverty', pp. 3–4.
91 See, for example, reviews by M. B. Katz, *The Undeserving Poor: From the War on Poverty to the War on Welfare*, Pantheon, 1989; H. Dean and P. Taylor-Gooby, 'Culture, Structure and Failure: The Underclass Debate', in *Dependency Culture*, Harvester, 1992; and L. Morris, *Dangerous Classes: The Underclass and Social Citizenship*, Routledge, 1994.
92 Dean and Taylor-Gooby, ibid.
93 Katz, *The Undeserving Poor*, p. 195.
94 Katz, *The Undeserving Poor*; Morris, *Dangerous Classes*.
95 Morris, ibid.
96 Cited by Katz, *The Undeserving Poor*.
97 F. Field, *Losing Out*, Blackwell, 1989.
98 See p. 17.
99 J. Essen and P. Wedge, *Continuities in Childhood Disadvantage*, Heinemann, 1982.
100 D. Pilling, *Escape From Disadvantage*, Falmer Press, 1990.
101 For example, studies by Heath, 1992, and Bradshaw and Holmes, 1989, both cited by Oppenheim, *Poverty: The Facts*. There is also evidence that lone mothers would want to work if their children were looked after adequately, for example studies cited by Kumar, *Poverty and Inequality*, p. 67, and Morris, *Dangerous Classes*, p. 126, and of the importance of the breadwinner role for men who are unemployed, for example, Morris, ibid., pp. 127–9.

2. The Decline of British Capital

Keith Gibbard

WHEN ENGELS WROTE *The Condition* Britain was entering the second phase of industrialisation, on the path to full maturity as an industrial nation. Developments in shipbuilding, engineering and heavy machinery were consolidating and extending its early lead, whilst the railway 'mania' of the late 1840s was about to give a massive stimulus to the all-round development of the British economy. By mid-century, Britain was producing around two-thirds of the world's coal, a half of all iron and a half of all cotton cloth, its position in world markets apparently unassailable. Engels provides us with a vivid picture of the beginnings of this transformation, and its impact upon the English working class. But with remarkable foresight he not only captures the essential features of this period of Britain's ascendancy to the status of workshop of the world. He also looks beyond to a very different epoch:

> German manufacturing is now making great efforts, and that of America has developed with giant strides. America, with its un-measured coal and iron fields, with its unexampled wealth of water-power and its navigable rivers, but especially with its energetic, active population, in comparison with which the English are phleg-matic dawdlers, – America has in less than ten years created a manufacture which already competes with England in the coarser cotton goods, has excluded the English from the markets of north and south America, and holds its own in China, side by side with England. If any country is adapted to holding a monopoly of manu-facture, it is America. (4: 579–80)

Here, in 1844, Engels anticipates in all essentials the terms of rivalry between the emerging capitalist nations, with its inevitable counter-part, the decline of British economic power. This chapter will examine that historical process. Following Engels's lead the principal focus will be upon the impact of the external challenge to British supremacy from the competing imperial nations, rather than the purely internal and domestic factors which lie behind British capital's weakness.

Of course any attempt to trace the trajectory of the British economy and society must include an account of its internal development, the historical process of class formation and dissolution. But the nature of that process raises theoretical issues which cannot be settled simply by recourse to a listing of the purely domestic historical problems. Thus, to take one example, in their study of the decline of the British economy, Elbaum and Lazonick, whilst rightly rejecting the view of economic orthodoxy that decline is simply due to the presence of market 'imperfections', proceed to elaborate an 'institutional' perspective in which:

> Entrenched institutional structures – including the structures of industrial relations, industrial organisation, educational systems, financial inter-mediation, international trade, and state-enterprise relations – constrained the ability of individuals, groups or corporate entities to transform the productive system.[1]

It is a familiar list, and its contents form the basis for a widespread literature on the subject of 'Britain's decline', but the method is essentially no different from that of the free-market theories that the authors seek to refute. The unspoken assumption is that the normal course of capitalist development is one of smooth, long-run equilibrium growth. Deviations from that path are then seen as the product of frictions operating within society to inhibit the process of capital accumulation. The fact that all human societies are subject to a cycle of growth, maturity and decline and that the accumulation of capital is contradictory, necessarily prone to interruptions, periods of crisis and conflicts between classes and nations, is set aside and ignored.

What these approaches lack is any conception of the decline of British capital as the outcome of a process of rivalry between the major economic powers, a system of imperialist states mutually interacting, alternating between periods of relative stability and those of open economic, political and military conflict. British social development has been determined and shaped above all by the fact of Britain's world position and the sapping of its strength as an imperialist power. Capital exists and can only exist as 'many capitals'. In the imperialist epoch this requires an understanding of national and international capital in its interconnectedness. As Trotsky reminded us more than 60 years ago:

> Marxism takes its point of departure from world economy, not as a sum of national parts but as a mighty and independent reality which has been created by the international division of labour and the world market, and which in our epoch imperiously dominates the national markets.[2]

Any attempt to explain the decline of British capital predominantly within a national framework must rely on an increasingly impoverished methodology.

It was the growing imperialist rivalry of the late nineteenth century which exposed the limits to the dominance of British capital. A fall in its share of world markets had become inevitable, although in ruling circles rivalry and decline were increasingly seen as two sides of the same coin. A Royal Commission appointed to inquire into the depression of trade and industry reported in 1886:

> We are beginning to feel the effects of foreign competition in quarters where our trade formerly enjoyed a practical monopoly ... In every quarter of the world the perseverance and enterprise of the Germans are making themselves felt.[3]

The relative decline in Britain's position, interwoven with the perceived loss of imperial power, produced a sense of absolute decline amounting to a crisis whatever the true position at that time. In Lord Randolph Churchill's apocalyptic vision the problems facing British industry were not of internal origin: 'You find foreign iron, foreign wool, foreign silk and cotton pouring into the country, flooding you, drowning you, sinking you, swamping you ...'[4]

Undoubtedly, British capital was losing ground, not only in terms of market share but also in productivity and technique, particularly in the newer industries. But as the symptoms of the crisis appeared in the form of overproduction and glutted markets, it would be quite misleading to view Britain simply as a passive victim of her rivals' success. Thus, for example, in the period 1880 to 1900 Britain's share of world steel output fell from one-third to one-seventh but this fact must be measured against an increase in British steel production of almost 500 per cent during the same period, a prodigious rate of growth. The slippage in Britain's position in the world economy should not obscure the fact that British capital was contributing in full measure in sowing the seeds of the first major crisis of imperialism. Those who would explain British decline in terms of the growing relative inefficiency of productive technique alone, are apt to forget that this took place against the background of an all-round development of the productive forces which was driving imperialism beyond all limited, national boundaries. The determining feature of this period was an increasingly bitter trade rivalry, driven by the overproduction of capital, in a whole spectrum of industries and markets both domestic and overseas. A popular journal at the time expressed this fact:

> Is there a mine to exploit, a railway to build, a native to convert from bread-fruit to tinned meat, from temperance to trade gin,

the German and the Englishman are struggling to be first. A million petty disputes build up the greatest cause of war the world has ever seen.[5]

Any attempt to chart the relatively poorer performance of British industry through a simple comparison of economic indicators in the various capitalist countries, outside of a framework which recognises that conflict and rivalry, winners and losers, are at the heart of the process will inevitably produce a misleading picture with the focus on purely internal domestic factors.

Chief among such explanations has been the role of the City, which, by acting as a channel for the export of capital in the late nineteenth century, is seen as having diverted funds from the task of expanding and modernising domestic industry. Through a long historical process, the City is viewed as having developed a separate and distinctive identity within the British class structure, aristocratic and aloof from business, its activities predominantly mercantile and commercial, its focus largely on overseas lending, rather than on the provision of finance for the accumulation of domestic capital in productive industry. Thus, in place of Lenin's classic model of 'finance capital' – involving the coalescence of banks and industry – there developed instead a crucial disjuncture between the two fractions of capital, with the City dominating state policy through its close links with the Bank of England and the Treasury.

A number of serious qualifications need to be made to this thesis however. Firstly, it rests upon a highly simplistic reading of Lenin's work in which the purely organisational aspects of the connection between finance and industry are highlighted. As one recent author has more accurately characterised Lenin's argument:

> [T]he concept of finance capital embraced a dichotomy: on the one hand, convergence between bank and industrial capital, on the other, the increasing separation between money capital and productive capital. In other words Lenin emphasised the distinction between the organisational and the economic relations of finance capital. Banking and industrial capital converge to create a powerful and in the end dominant oligarchy of finance capitalists, and yet remain separate and relatively autonomous circuits of capital.[6]

Thus new forms of credit and finance, characteristic of imperialism, made possible a growing separation, both spatially and temporally, between the circuits of money and productive capital. But this took place through a growing trend towards monopoly capital in which industry and financial institutions were ever more closely enmeshed. The interests of money and productive capital in Britain were certainly not identical during this period, but to suggest that the City was dissociated from production is fanciful. The maintenance of an unchanged value of sterling under the nineteenth-century gold standard, the basis of the City's standing as the world's banker, would have been impossible without the dominating influence of British industry in world trade. Indeed the export of capital through the City served not only to enlarge the markets for industry but also ensured a continuing supply of cheap raw materials for its factories. The further argument that British industry was starved of the funds required to modernise in order to face the threat from its emerging rivals remains unproven. Recent studies suggest that until 1914 there was little demand for such funds from industry, particularly from the old staple industries such as coal, iron and steel, and textiles.

Those who have held the City responsible for the failure of the new industries which developed in the late nineteenth century have typically done so by contrasting them with their more powerful rivals. Germany is taken as the archetypal case where bank support for industry supposedly contrasted sharply with British experience. This simplistic conclusion requires some qualification. Whilst some sections of the German electrical industry, for example, developed under the close supervision of the big banks, other family-owned companies, notably Siemens, retained greater independence. Similarly, the German chemical industry developed with little support from the banks, as in Britain. Indeed the evidence does not support a picture of the role of banking capital as the key to German industrial success. As late as 1928 the lion's share of bank credit in that country was being channelled into the older staple industries, the two biggest recipients being textiles with 11.8 per cent and food with 11.2 per cent, against only 3.6 per cent for the chemical industry and 2.9 per cent for engineering and automobile construction.[7]

The view that British economic failure stemmed from the late or incomplete development of finance capital is not borne out by the evidence. The development of British banking did not lag behind in the move towards monopoly and the centralisation of capital. Already, by the eve of the First World War, a dozen banks based in London with a country-wide network of branches, controlled around two-thirds of the deposits of England and Wales. The trend continued after the war with the emergence of the 'big five' which by 1938 controlled some 90 per cent of the deposits of the country. In contrast, the share of the deposits of the big Berlin banks never exceeded 30 per cent until the Second World War.

If there are serious objections to the argument that it was the absence of finance capital in Britain which lay behind her economic weakness in this period, we should be equally cautious of the simplistic view on policy. As the over-accumulation of capital led to intensified competition between capitalist states, protectionism grew in international trade relations. According to the conventional wisdom, the City's continuing adherence to international free trade and the defeat of Joseph Chamberlain's bid to introduce a measure of protection for industry through tariff reform, beginning in 1897, crucially prevented the restructuring and cartelisation of industry which was taking place in Germany and the US. Certainly British capital was divided on the issue of free trade versus protection but it was not along clear-cut, City versus industry lines. Free trade found its supporters not only in the City but also in key sectors of industry, whilst leading City merchant houses, including Hambros and Rothschild, supported Chamberlain's campaign.

When war came it was widely seen in ruling-class circles as an opportunity to restore Britain's flagging economy and to reassert the position of British capital within world imperialism. According to a *Daily Telegraph* leader in August 1914:

> This war provides our businessmen with such an opportunity as has never come their way before ... There is no reason why we should not permanently seize for this country a large proportion of Germany's export trade.[8]

In fact British manufacturers lost markets throughout the war, the principal beneficiary being the US. Between 1913 and 1920 the US share of world exports rose dramatically from 13.5 per cent to over 25 per cent. Whilst engaged in a barbaric conflict with one imperialist rival in the military sphere, Britain's position in the economic sphere was being irrevocably undermined. Indeed by late 1918, the British Government was forced to slow down the shipment of American troops to the battlefield in order to release British shipping to counter US trade competition in overseas markets.[9]

The erosion of Britain's supremacy in world markets was mirrored in the country's financial position. Prior to the war, Britain, with 44 per cent of global overseas assets, had foreign holdings in excess of those of the US, Germany and France combined. Britain's war expenditure, estimated at over £9½ billion led to a wholesale liquidation of that capital. British investors' holdings of saleable foreign securities, such as American stocks and bonds, were requisitioned by the government and sold to swell foreign exchange reserves. Altogether some £1 billion of Britain's foreign investments were liquidated, a quarter of the total. Increasingly Britain was forced to turn to America's sceptical banking system for financial support via the British government's agents in New York, J. P. Morgan and Company. In July 1917, Foreign Secretary Balfour cabled the White House:

We seem to be on the verge of a financial disaster that would be worse than defeat in the field. If we cannot keep up exchange, neither we nor our allies can pay our dollar debts. We should be driven off the gold basis, purchases from USA would immediately cease, and the Allies' credit would be shattered ... you know I am not an alarmist but this is really serious.[10]

The impact of war had thus transformed the relative positions of British and American imperialism. In a public statement, issued in 1916, the US Federal Reserve, warning American banks not to extend too much credit to Britain, wrote that:

The United States has now attained a position of wealth and international financial power, which, in the natural course of events, it could not have reached for a generation. We must be careful not to impair this position of strength and independence.[11]

Between 1900 and 1920, the US went from a position of relative international insignificance to one of predominance. A major international borrower and recipient of foreign direct investment before 1900, by 1920 the US had emerged as the world's leading new lender and foreign direct investor. British imperialism, by contrast, emerged from the war burdened by debt, the economy seriously debilitated. Prior to the war, London had been the principal centre of the international gold standard. A surplus on the current account of the balance of payments in almost every year in the century prior to 1914, ensured by large invisible earnings, had meant that the country could simultaneously maintain a fixed gold/sterling exchange rate and relatively easy credit conditions domestically, whilst acting as banker to the world through overseas loans. Under these conditions there was no objective conflict of interest between City and industry. That conflict developed only after the war and as a result of the colossal damage done to Britain's standing as an imperialist power. Having borrowed $3.7 billion from the US, whilst inflating the domestic note issue nearly ten-fold in the course of the war, the post-war attempt to restore the gold standard at the pre-war parity could only take place under savagely deflationary conditions, with severe damage to Britain's outdated manufacturing base. But, to repeat, this was not due to some peculiarity of Britain's internal class development – the aristocratic coloration of the City, an archaic culture hostile to industry. It was the outcome of the first major encounter between the great imperial powers in which British imperialism emerged as the military victor in the battle against one rival, only to lose the economic war against the other.

Certainly the restoration of the gold standard in 1925 was the policy of the City, the Treasury and the bankers who drafted the influential

Cunliffe Committee report. The ability of the pound to 'look the dollar in the eye' once more was thought crucial to the continuation of London as a centre of world finance. But opposition from industry was muted, certainly stopping well short of a City–industry split. Possibly, industrialists recognised that while the deflationary policies introduced in 1920, necessary to restore the value of sterling, made British goods even more uncompetitive on world markets, those same policies, by sharply driving up unemployment, were instrumental in heading off the massive wave of strikes which followed the end of the war. Where criticism came, there was a clear recognition that the real threat to British industry was not the dominance of the City but the growing power of American capital. As Sir Alfred Mond, Chairman of the UK chemicals firm Brunner Mond, famously expressed the position:

> Now, apparently, we are to be harnessed to the money rate in New York, our trade to be further depressed whenever there is a flurry on Wall Street, because some people think that we must be hanged on a cross of gold ... I can imagine nothing more dangerous to the harassed and already depressed trade of this country than that we should hitch ourselves on to the American money market, and take it as the guide and goal and lodestar of British finance.[12]

In fact the restoration lasted just six short years with Britain leading the world off the gold standard in 1931 under the combined forces of the US depression and the collapse of the German banking system. It was a move widely seen as a *de facto* repudiation of Britain's unsupportable war debts. In the decade and a half following the 1918 Armistice, servicing of the debt had called for an annual sum roughly equivalent to almost double pre-war government expenditure.

The inter-war period as a whole witnessed a consolidation of finance capital in Britain. Merchant banks and investment trusts which had previously devoted themselves almost entirely to overseas activities paid increasing attention to the financing of domestic industry. Such eminent City establishments as Rothschilds, Baring Brothers, Morgan Grenfell, Lazards and Kleinwort turned to the issue of domestic non-governmental securities during the 1920s and 1930s, whilst the big clearing banks were extending ever larger facilities to British manufacturing – 'a marriage between the industry of the north and the finance of the south', as the Governor of the Bank of England expressed it in 1930.[13] The merger wave following the war certainly did not 'solve' the problem of the old staple industries – British capital's inheritance as first industrial nation – but nor was the competitive performance of British manufacturing during this period a simple tale of decline relative to other capitalist nations. The period from the closing years of the First World War to the early 1930s saw a significant restructuring of British manufacturing industry. Large firms were consolidating their hold on the economy, raising their share of manufacturing output by as much as nine percentage points from 17 per cent in 1919 to 26 per cent in 1930, a rate not exceeded since. Between 1920 and 1930, one-third of gross capital formation was directed to five major growth industries: rayon, electricals, motors, chemicals and paper. Indeed, throughout the inter-war period the rate of growth of industrial production in Britain matched and even exceeded that in Germany,[14] whilst as a result of the concentration and centralisation of capital, Britain's 100 largest industrial firms by the mid-1920s accounted for approximately the same share of domestic manufacturing output as did the 100 largest American companies. The consolidation of finance capital also witnessed the first major steps towards multinational production. In the chemical industry, ICI formed a patent sharing arrangement with Du Pont of America and IG Farben of Germany, based upon a general agreement to divide the world market between themselves. By 1930, four of the largest firms in Britain – Ford, AEI, Boots and International Nickel – were under North American ownership. Whereas in 1914 there had been some 70 US companies operating in the UK, by 1936 this had risen to 224, many of them among the dominant firms in their industry. Similarly, many of the larger British firms developed new overseas subsidiaries during this period. By 1934, for example, British firms had acquired assets in US manufacturing valued at $305 million. Thus the nature and structure of finance capital which emerged in Britain in this period, based upon the growth of the large corporation and the transition from competitive to monopoly capital, was essentially no different from that in the other major imperialist countries. In particular, the early acceptance of the role of multinational capital was a signpost of future trends within British capital.

The Second World War finally established beyond doubt the ascendancy of the US as the leading imperialist power. Leo D. Welch, Treasurer of Standard Oil of New Jersey, confidently asserted in 1946:

As the largest producer, the largest source of capital, and the biggest contributor to the global mechanism, we must set the pace and assume the responsibility of the major stockholder in this corporation known as the world.[15]

British dependence on American financial, material and military support in the course of the war crucially shaped the political economy of British capital in the whole post-war period. War itself had forced sales of British foreign assets in excess of £1 billion, a net reduction in gold and dollar reserves of £152 million and an increase in overseas debts of almost £3 billion. Taking into account physical destruction and disinvestment within Britain, a rough estimate, produced during the American loan negotiations in 1945, suggested that a quarter of British capital had been lost. By the end of the war, depleted gold and foreign currency reserves of £610 millions were dwarfed by external liabilities in excess of £3.5 billion, two-thirds of which were held in the 'sterling area'. It was this factor above all others which explains the continuing fragility of sterling in the postwar decades, and the intermittent recourse to bouts of deflation or 'stop-go' policies, with their attendant attacks on working-class living standards, in an attempt to defend the value of the pound. The undermining of sterling's role as an international currency was not simply a monetary question however. It reflected a sea change in the position of British imperialism in the world economy and its relationship to the rival capitalist powers.

The Lend Lease arrangement during the war, whereby US capital underwrote the British war effort, presaged what was to come. If US business had been prepared to help finance Britain's war against German expansion it was anxious not to strengthen British world ambitions in the process. One US general, for example, objected to weapons purchased under Lend Lease being used to recapture Hong Kong and thus consolidate the British Empire. Under the terms of the Lend Lease agreement, British exports were to stop competing with American exports and Britain was forced to agree to abandon the system of imperial preference and adopt a policy of free trade at the end of the war. Thus, British capital found itself in a hopelessly contradictory position, fighting a war to cling on to its colonial possessions whilst accepting terms which would effectively undermine the whole economic basis of its colonial system. With the abrupt ending of Lend Lease in 1945, the incoming Labour government in dire financial straits turned to the US for a loan. The British Chancellor, Hugh Dalton, captured the atmosphere of the loan negotiation between the two imperialist powers:

> So, as the talks went on, we retreated slowly and with bad grace and with increasing irritation, from a free gift to an interest free loan, and from this again to a loan bearing interest; from a larger to a smaller total of aid; and from the prospect of loose strings, some of which would be only general declarations of intention to the most unwilling acceptance of strings so tight they might strangle our trade and, indeed, our whole economic life.[16]

The conditions attached to the loan included an acceptance by Britain of the terms of the Bretton Woods agreement, which sanctified the dollar as the principal currency in world trade, the elimination of protectionism, the ending of restrictions on US imports by the end of

1946 and full sterling convertibility by July 1947. The House of Commons was allowed five days to accept or reject the package. As one MP speaking in the debate commented, a visitor from Mars 'might well be pardoned for thinking that he was listening to the representatives of a vanquished people discussing the economic penalties of defeat'.[17] In practice the overwhelming demands on the British economy led to the exhaustion of the loan within 18 months, whilst the continuing dependence on US imports and the consequent dollar deficit led to the suspension of sterling convertibility within months of its introduction in 1947, followed by a massive sterling devaluation two years later. The emergency austerity Budget in the autumn of 1947, in an attempt to bridge the gap in overseas payments at a time when the rest of the capitalist world was beginning to experience the benefits of post-war expansion, set the tone for years to follow. The resigned acceptance of a sterling devaluation from \$4.03 to \$2.80 was a symbolic measure of the changed situation compared to the end of the First World War when British capital had fought to re-establish the gold standard at the pre-war parity.

A principal factor in the declining relative strength of British industry in the post-war years was the political attempt to sustain a global military presence and the fiction of an equal relationship with US imperialism when the economic conditions for such a role had been completely undermined. Keynes, Britain's chief negotiator, had already recognised that:

> It comes out in the wash that the American loan is primarily required to meet the political and military expenditure overseas. If it were not for that, we could scrape through without excessive interruption of our domestic programme.[18]

Between 1947 and 1950, cuts in defence spending, combined with sterling devaluation and a general increase in world trade, appeared to produce the beginnings of economic revival in Britain. In fact the nature of the recovery demonstrated the extent to which British capital was strategically still reliant on empire. Initially, the outbreak of the Korean War in 1950 led to a world-wide boom in raw material prices due to American stock building. The rapid rise in rubber and tin prices solved at a stroke the problem of the dollar deficit with the US via Britain's imperial interests in Malaya. In 1950, Malayan exports to the US alone more than covered the UK dollar deficit on current account. Indeed, by 1951, Malayan tin and rubber earned more American dollars for Britain than the total of British dollar exports. In response to US demands at the outbreak of the Korean War, however, the Attlee government launched a massive rearmament programme involving a doubling of defence expenditure for the years 1951–54, channelling resources away from civilian and into military production. As overseas raw material prices fell back again with the end of the war, Britain's sources of colonial revenue shrank and the balance of payments went into a sharp deficit, leading to further deflation and an actual fall in manufacturing output and GNP in 1952. The first major breach in post-war growth was thus the combined result of global commitments far in excess of those undertaken by any of Britain's major capitalist rivals, in an attempt to preserve the semblance of an increasingly costly colonial role. Through the early 1950s, British military production exceeded that of all of the other European NATO partners combined.

The whole period demonstrated both the economic impact of the Labour government's attempt to sustain the pre-war status of British imperialism as well as the British economy's dependence on a colonial pattern of trade and international payments which was no longer viable, and which was to be effectively destroyed in the wave of anti-colonial struggles which swept across Africa and Asia in the post-war period.

TABLE 2.1 *Overseas Capital Investments of Britain and the US.*

	1939	1949
US (£ m)	2,500	11,650
UK (£ m)	3,545	1,960

The clearest expression of the changed fortunes of British and US imperialism can be seen in their respective amounts of overseas capital (see Table 2.1)[19] The growth in US overseas investment was particularly targeted at Britain and its traditional areas of influence. Thus, by the end of 1953, American investment in the British Commonwealth amounted to 43 per cent of all US foreign investment. In oil, the key raw material in the post-war period, the US gradually displaced British imperialism's leading position in the Middle East. It was part of a broader pattern in which, for example, US access to strategic raw materials in the colonies of the European powers was made a key condition upon receipt of Marshall Aid. But it was in Britain itself that US investment was to have its greatest impact as American multinationals rapidly spread their influence in Europe. Between 1950 and 1967 investment by US corporations in

European manufacturing and mining industries rose more than ten-fold, from $1,358 million to $14,185 million. with the lion's share, almost two-thirds, going to Britain. The investment was concentrated in the more technologically advanced industries: chemicals, mechanical and electrical engineering, and above all motor vehicles.

The car industry in particular developed after the Second World War as the key industrial sector, the hallmark of manufacturing success or failure in the leading capitalist states. But the relationship between the state and the auto industry in Britain was in marked contrast to that in the other leading European nations. In West Germany, for example, the post-war development of the car industry saw a continuation of the close relationship between state and auto capital which had developed in the fascist period, as the Bonn Republic sustained the clear difference of treatment between domestic producers, notably Volkswagen, and foreign car manufacturers. Whilst a small number of core domestic producers were nurtured by the German state and ensured continuing supplies of vital raw materials and cheap labour, the US multinationals, Ford and Opel (a subsidiary of General Motors), were increasingly relegated to the periphery.[20] In Britain, by contrast, US multinational capital was welcomed and treated on equal terms with the domestic industry, quickly growing to dominate it. Thus, by the 1950s Ford's assets in Britain, which in 1929 were below those of either Morris or Austin, Britain's leading car producers, had outstripped their combined asset value. Support by the British state for the expansion of the US multinationals in the immediate post-war period was closely tied to the need to increase exports and close the dollar gap at all costs. As a result, the British share of world motor exports rose from 15 per cent in 1937 to 52 per cent in 1950, becoming for a brief period the world's leading car exporting nation, with Ford as Britain's principal exporter.[21] Indeed, at the outbreak of the Korean War in 1950, Ford were exempted from the steel quotas which were imposed upon domestic manufacturers. In the short term, the policy of the British government towards multinational capital thus appeared to be successful but the longer term consequences for the indigenous auto industry were disastrous. Unable to reap the benefits of scale economies in its own domestic market, enjoyed by the other major continental producers, and left to compete with the far larger US multinationals, the position of the domestic car producers suffered a continual decline.

By 1967, Ford, following the logic of multinational capital, had introduced the idea of the European car. The other US producers, Chrysler and General Motors, adopted the same policy soon after. The change was to have serious implications for Britain's trade balance, as a growing share of components were sourced from abroad. From being a vital part of the drive for exports in the post-war years, Ford and General Motors were together, by the early 1980s, adding some £1.3 billion to the British trade deficit as a result of these tied imports.

The post-war legacy of Britain's imperial role, its colonial, financial and military connections around the globe, and the connected weakness of its productive capital, led naturally to the disproportionate influence of multinational capital, both British and foreign owned, in the UK economy. By 1970, all of the top 100 British manufacturing companies had become multinationals and despite having a much smaller and weaker overall industrial base than Germany, 11 of the world's 100 largest businesses were British, compared with 18 for the rest of the EEC. Among the 200 largest non-American companies, 53 were British, 43 Japanese, 25 German and 23 French. At the same time, the value of foreign production by British business was more than double the value of visible exports, whereas it was less than 40 per cent for Germany and Japan. As one commentator, reflecting on this period, has noted:

> The result of the renewal of Britain's traditional liberal orientation to the world economy was that a serious conflict began to develop between the international priorities of British policy and the needs of the domestic economy. This was sometimes presented as a new clash between manufacturing industry and the financial sector. But the real clash was between the new and often combined international operations of British industry and British finance, and the requirements of domestic expansion.[22]

The growing influence of multinationals in Britain was matched by parallel changes in the nature of the City itself. International production required more flexibility in capital and currency markets, which commenced with the development of the Eurodollar market.[23] International banks based in London had held dollar balances outside the US as early as the inter-war period, but it was not until the early 1960s that the market took on real significance. Driven by US inflationary financing of the Vietnam War, with its concomitant balance of payments deficits, growing dollar balances held abroad offered new opportunities for both borrowers and lenders. For banks and investors, Eurocurrencies were a method of evading the monetary controls and credit policies of central banks and national governments. Thus the London Eurodollar market was totally free from US Federal Reserve restrictions, whilst US and other multinationals based in Europe could find an assured source of easy credit, whatever the current monetary policy of the host nation. By 1966, US firms were borrowing around $500 million from the Eurodollar market. The fact that such large currency balances had developed outside the control of any domestic monetary authority gave a massive boost to speculative trading. The sterling crises of the Wilson government, culminating in the 1967 sterling devaluation, were a clear testimony to the inability of the British state to pursue Keynesian-type policies based upon purely domestic considerations in a world increasingly dominated by international capital. The terms for securing IMF support for the devaluation included cuts in public expenditure and the beginning of attempts to control the money stock, whilst as Wilson's own account of the period makes clear, the shock of sterling's fall stiffened the resolve of the government to legislate against the strength of the trade unions. In a bout of collective amnesia these same policies were later to be presented by some commentators as constituting the core of 'Thatcherism'.

What is clear, however, is that Britain's currency difficulties reflected not merely the relative weakness of the UK economy but foreshadowed the break-up of the whole Bretton Woods system of fixed exchange rates as the period of post-war capitalist expansion came to an end. The subsequent global recession has dominated the recent history of the British economy with the relative decline in its manufacturing base becoming absolute. Thus between 1973 and 1982, manufacturing output actually fell by 18 per cent, leading in 1983 to the first UK trade deficit in manufactures since the Industrial Revolution. Much of that decline was concentrated in the first years of the Thatcher administration as a result of a deliberate policy of savage deflation, aimed at weakening the power of the organised working class whilst eradicating the weaker, uncompetitive fractions of small- and medium-sized capital. A surplus on trade in manufactures of £5 billion in 1980 had become a deficit of £4 billion by 1985, whilst at the height of the onslaught in 1982, company liquidations reached a record 12,000, with unemployment rising to over three million. Ian McGregor, appropriately a partner in the Wall Street firm, Lazard Bros, was typical of the managers brought in by Thatcher to oversee the process. After breaking the steel strike in 1980, McGregor proceeded to reduce the British Steel workforce from 168,000 to 78,000 before moving on to decimate the coal industry.[24] In the same period, employment at British Leyland was reduced by 53 per cent, whilst major private firms such as Courtaulds, Tube Investments, Dunlop and Talbot each cut their workforce by more than 50 per cent.

These developments were paralleled by rapid changes within the City of London. Thatcher's immediate abolition of all controls on capital movements, on taking office in 1979, the growth and proliferation of new forms of speculative finance, fuelled in particular by the petrodollars let loose by the second oil price hike in that year, through to full deregulation of the City following 'Big Bang' in 1986, formed part of a global expansion in financial markets and the creation of new forms of fictitious capital. UK capital exports, around £600 million in the early 1970s, reached levels in excess of

£10 billion in 1981.[25] These developments have led an array of commentators into reviving, unamended, the notion of a split within British capital between City and industry, with the former supposedly prospering at the expense of the latter. It is a thesis which completely misreads the real nature of finance capital in this period. For the dominant feature is the development of truly multinational capital in which the circuits of money and productive capital are ever more closely intertwined. This drawing together of finance and industry is accelerated at times of crisis. The banks and other big financial institutions play a more active role in the centralisation of capital by facilitating mergers and take-overs, with the power to decide which companies will be liquidated and which supplied with additional credit. Nor is this process confined to the productive sections of capital. The financial institutions are involved in the same predatory process amongst themselves.

Britain, as we have seen, was at the forefront of the development of multinational capital, at first operating in the sphere of production. By 1959, for example, no less than 700 US multinationals had a UK subsidiary at a time when only seven US banks were located in London. The subsequent growth of new forms of international financial markets and instruments was in large part a response to the globalisation of production relations and the possibility of extracting a share of surplus value through mere financial manipulation. But this was by no means a purely British phenomenon. At the end of the 1970s it is estimated that the liquid assets of all forms of multinational capital had reached around three times the size of the world's gold and foreign exchange reserves. Far from being a passive victim of monetary speculation, large-scale industrial capital has increasingly coalesced with finance, threatening in the process the survival of smaller, localised fractions of capital. Thus in Britain, for example, the large financial institutions increased their holdings of all quoted ordinary shares of UK companies from about 18 per cent in 1957 to 40 per cent by 1973. This tendency of the merging of industry and finance, which forms according to Lenin the history and content of the term 'finance capital', is central to an understanding of capitalism in Britain at the end of the twentieth century. Certainly there is a glaring contradiction in Britain's role as host to the largest foreign exchange market in the world whilst supplying no more than 4 per cent of global manufacturing output, but, to repeat, the impact has largely been upon small- and medium-sized domestically-based capital which has suffered the predations of multinational finance capital in all its forms. Simplistic attempts to conduct a debate over the British economy in national terms in which industry and the City are identified as victim and villain can only lead to reactionary conclusions in this period. Those who still cling to the notion of the City as an aristocratic enclave, indifferent to the needs of British industry, completely misrepresent the nature of Thatcher's project in the 1980s. Instinctively hostile to 'gentlemanly capitalism', Thatcher forced aside the patrician element in the Tory Party. With the deep recession of the early 1980s, contributions to Tory Party funds from traditional sources within British manufacturing shrank, to be replaced by donors representing large-scale monopoly capital – the big construction firms, retail and food groups, and multinational holding companies.

At the same time the composition of the institutions located in the City underwent a fundamental change. Whilst London retained its status as an international financial centre, it came to be increasingly dominated by overseas banks. By 1983, some 400 foreign banks were directly represented in the City, with Japanese banks emerging as the biggest London-based lenders, ahead of their British and US counterparts. The internationalisation of capital has advanced to the point where it becomes increasingly problematic to state clearly what is meant by the 'UK Economy'. Around one-quarter of UK GNP is now produced by foreign multinationals, whilst the leading 50 British manufacturing companies produce 44 per cent of their output from overseas subsidiaries. What is clear is that 'economic success' as measured by the profitability of multi-national finance capital has only a limited connection with the health of the national economy as conventionally defined.

With the contraction of the manufacturing sector, some commentators have held out the prospect of a transition to a post-industrial 'service' economy in Britain. The development of the service sector is not a new phenomenon. Indeed, at no time since the Second World War has manufacturing industry employed as many workers as in services. The past 15 years have nonetheless witnessed a growth in particular areas, notably finance, telecommunications, retail and leisure, as well as the privatised public utilities. These industries however have been brought firmly under the control of finance capital and in that respect are subject to exactly the same 'rules of the game' as manufacturing. The conglomerate British American Tobacco (BAT), for example, in addition to its production activities, has ownership of City-based financial institutions as well as interests in a large retail and distribution chain. To describe these developments as a move towards a 'post-industrial' economy is simply to confuse the process at work. New areas of social life, culture, recreation and leisure, have been commodified, whilst basic public services including water, health and public housing have been drawn over the fateful threshold of exchange value. Multinational capital has shifted into these sectors partly as a result of the greater degree of monopoly and the fact that they are relatively protected from international competition, allowing higher profits to be made. In addition, the service industries have allowed the recruitment of unorganised sections of the working class where the rate of exploitation is higher. By 1984, almost 90 per cent of Britain's part-time workers were in services, the majority of them women in low-paid jobs. Whilst the shrinkage of manufacturing has been pronounced in Britain, it is a development common to all of the advanced capitalist states. New labour-saving technologies combined with the relocation of production to the former colonial 'newly industrialised' countries, where finance capital can find readily available pools of cheap labour, are creating the same conditions of mass unemployment and 'de-industrialisation' in all of the old centres of manufacturing.

The beginning of the decline of British capital coincided with the birth of the epoch of imperialism in the late nineteenth century. As the leading imperial power, Britain was of necessity fully engaged in the storms and upheavals to which that system has given rise. As a result, Britain's history in the past century reflects the contradictory history of imperialism as a whole, perhaps more than any other nation. From economic rivalry through trade wars to all out military conflict, British capital and British class relations have been shaped and moulded in the image of imperialism. Britain's historical legacy, its position for centuries at the hub of a network of colonial relations across the globe, crucially influenced the outlook and polity of the British ruling class in response to these challenges. But that influence was not through the retention of archaic, anti-capitalist institutions which limited the modernisation of domestic industry. On the contrary, in a failed attempt to sustain its global influence, the British capitalist class in the twentieth century has embraced the development of finance capital in all its 'modern' forms, from the early introduction of multinational firms, all the way through to more recent developments in shady arms dealing, collapsed banks and pension fund frauds. It has been a long held truism that within the capitalist world, the British economy was an aberration, out of step with its rivals. A victim of every possible malaise, its failure could be held out as a yardstick with which to measure the progress of the more 'normal' capitalist powers. In a world economy mired in a seemingly endless recession, dominated by footloose multinational capital, such a view is increasingly untenable. As the symptoms of the British disease – mass unemployment; growing state deficits and monetary instability – reappear in every corner of the international economy, it is more and more the case that, whilst Britain is leading the process of decline, its position is not as 'exceptional' as some have argued. Indeed the policies pursued by the Thatcher government throughout the 1980s in response to the decline of British capital – tighter monetary controls, cuts in state expenditure, the privatisation of public enterprises and the creation of 'flexible labour markets' through attacks on the rights and institutions of the working class – have been almost universally adopted with greater or lesser enthusiasm. In one report after another they now form the official policy of the whole of the OECD, the World Bank and the International Monetary Fund.

Engels wrote his classic study on the very eve of Britain's emergence as the dominant industrial power in the world. Not least among the many qualities of his work was the recognition that the near-monopoly position Britain was to establish in the world could not last indefinitely. As we near the end of the twentieth century, that monopoly position – and all the privileges it brought, not least for a minority of the working class – is now certainly over. This decline in the British economy, as part of the growing crisis of capitalism as a whole, involves social and political consequences of similar, if not greater, significance than those examined by Engels 150 years ago.

Notes

1 B. Elbaum and W. Lazonick, 'The Decline of the British Economy: An Institutional Perspective', *Journal of Economic History*, vol. LXIV, no. 2, pp. 567–83, p. 568.

2 L. D. Trotsky, *The Permanent Revolution*, Pathfinder, 1969, p. 146.

3 K. Hutchison, *The Decline and Fall of British Capitalism*, Anchor Books, 1951, p. 19.

4 Ibid., p. 20

5 *Saturday Review*, 11 September 1897, quoted in ibid., p. 103.

6 D. Nicholls, 'A Subordinate Bourgeoisie? The Question of Hegemony in British Capitalist Society', in C. Barker and D. Nicholls, (eds), *The Development of British Capitalist Society: A Marxist Debate*, Northern Marxist Historians Group, 1988, p. 57.

7 Y. Cassis, 'British Finance: Success and Controversy', in J. J. Van Helten and Y. Cassis, *Capitalism in a Mature Economy: Financial Institutions, Capital Exports and British Industry, 1870–1930*, Edward Elgar, 1990, p. 10.

8 Quoted in Hutchison, *The Decline and Fall of British Capitalism*, p. 159.

9 P. J. Cain and A. G. Hopkins, *British Imperialism, Crisis and Destruction, 1914–90*, Longman, 1993, p. 60.

10 Hutchison, *The Decline and Fall of British Capitalism*, p. 169.

11 J. M. Cooper, Jnr, 'The Command of Gold Reversed: American Loans to Britain, 1915–1917' *Pacific Historical Review*, no. 45, pp. 209–30, p. 222.

12 W. Adams Brown, Jnr, 'The Conflict of Opinion and Economic Interest in England', in S. Pollard (ed.), *The Gold Standard and Employment Policies Between the Wars*, Methuen, 1970, p. 55.

13 M. Dintenfass, *The Decline of Industrial Britain, 1870–1980*, Routledge, 1992, p. 44.

14 A. Sked, *Britain's Decline*, Blackwell, 1987, p. 24.

15 A. Carew, *Labour Under the Marshall Plan: the Politics of Productivity and the Marketing of Management Science*, Manchester University Press, 1987, p. 40.

16 E. A. Brett, *The World Economy Since the War: The Politics of Uneven Development*, Macmillan, 1985, p. 139.

17 J. C. R. Dow, *The Management of the British Economy 1945–60*, Cambridge Univerity Press, 1970, p. 18.

18 J. Fyrth, *Labour's High Noon: the Government and the Economy 1945–51*, Lawrence and Wishart, 1993, p. xxv.

19 Source: R. Palme Dutt, *The Crisis of Britain and the British Empire*, Lawrence and Wishart, 1953, p. 156.

20 See S. Reich, *The Fruits of Fascism: Post-war Prosperity in Historical Perspective*, Cornell University Press, 1990.

21 R. A. Church, *The Rise and Decline of the British Motor Industry*, Macmillan, 1994, p. 44.

22 A. Gamble, *Britain in Decline: Economic Policy and Political Strategy*, Macmillan, 1990, p. 111.

23 M. Hughes, 'American Investment in Britain', in J. Urry and J. Wakeford, (eds) *Power in Britain*, Heinemann Educational, 1973, p. 178.

24 H. Overbeek, *Global Capitalism and National Decline*, Unwin Hyman, 1990, p. 189.

25 J. Coakley, 'The Internationalisation of Bank Capital', *Capital and Class*, no. 23, p. 117.

3. Engels and the Industrial Revolution[1]

Geoff Pilling

IT IS A COMMONPLACE amongst historians, sociologists, political scientists and others that British history is unique, characterised as it is by a lack of sharp turning points and violent disjunctures. Such a view is held not simply by writers of a conservative disposition. Thus Perry Anderson and Tom Nairn have for long argued that it is the incompleteness of the bourgeois revolution, the lack of a thorough-going modernisation of the state in this country, that marks British history off from that of continental Europe.

Whatever can be said for such a position, it was not one shared by Frederick Engels. Coming to England as a young man in his early twenties, he witnessed a social transformation taking place that he regarded as far more profound than the changes then happening in France and Germany. In the industrial revolution, he saw something of far greater significance than for the city of Manchester and its surrounding towns; it was an event with truly universal implications. For the industrial revolution brought into being a quite new social class – the modern working class – and it was this more than anything that interested Engels. It was in *The Condition of the Working Class in England* that Engels demonstrated that this class was not simply a hopeless, trampled-down class but one that was forced to fight against the conditions into which it had been plunged. In so doing, Engels made a decisive contribution to the development of the materialist conception of history.

This chapter takes up this question of the nature and the consequences of the industrial revolution as part of a wider project: the rescuing of Engels, and Marx, from the fate that befell them after their deaths. Their creative work became distorted beyond belief, in part in the lifetime of the Second International, but above all in the period when the Stalinist bureaucracy ruled the Soviet Union and controlled a significant sector of the world's labour movement.

For most writers the 'industrial revolution', assuming the term retains any validity, has, especially in the recent past, been reduced to a series of technical changes in the sphere of production; either that, or to a discussion about rates of 'economic growth' in the late eighteenth and early nineteenth centuries. In this respect the *social* character of the revolution is lost sight of. This chapter lays no claim to be a historiography of the industrial revolution. Rather it sets out to consider certain methodological issues which are felt to be crucial if the real character of the changes that were taking place in England 150 years ago are to be understood. It attempts to rescue Engels's conception of the industrial revolution from a narrow, mechanistic mis-reading; for it was precisely because the changes Engels witnessed on his arrival in Manchester were part of a profound social upheaval that he was obliged to study how the consciousness of the working class was developing and would develop.

Looking back some 50 years after the first publication of *The Condition*, Engels had the following to say:

> It will hardly be necessary to point out that the general theoreti- cal standpoint of this book – philosophical, economical, political – does not exactly coincide with my standpoint of to-day. Modern international Socialism, since fully developed as a science, chiefly and almost exclusively through the efforts of Marx, did not yet exist in 1844. My book represents one of the phases of its embry- onic development; and as the human embryo, in its early stages, still reproduces the gill-arches of our fish-ancestors, so this book exhibits everywhere the traces of the descent of modern socialism from one of its ancestors, German philosophy.[2]

Engels was drawing attention to the fact that his work was part of that 'pre-history' of Marxism during which time both he and Marx were still developing the foundations of their new, revolutionary, world outlook. Any theoretical limitations in *The Condition* lay essentially in the fact that the critique of bourgeois economy ('Marx- ist economic theory') was still to be completed. This limitation is reflected in the first place in the fact that, at certain points, Engels asserts that the doctrine of communism transcends the contra- dictions between labour and capital, an idea which, in effect, stands in opposition to the thrust of the entire work. Engels came to this conclusion principally because certain members of the bourgeoisie were coming to realise the inevitability of socialism and were siding with the working class. Thus he writes towards the end of the work:

> ... as Communism stands above the strife between bourgeoisie and proletariat, it will be easier for the better elements of the bourgeoisie (which are, however, deplorably few, and we can look

for recruits only among the rising generation) to unite with it
than purely proletarian Chartism. (4: 582)[3]

Similar traces of the standpoint of utopian socialism are to be
seen in Engels's Hobbesian-like contention that society consists of
a war of all against all. He tended to see the basic contradiction
underlying this war in a manner not unlike that of the utopian
socialists, namely as: '[a] glaring contradiction between a few rich
people, on the one hand, and many poor on the other, a contradiction which has already risen to a menacing point in England
and France and is daily growing sharper in our country too'
(4: 243).

These limitations notwithstanding, Engels's work represented a
decisive step in the direction of Marxism, above all because it saw
in the modern working class, that force created by the industrial
revolution, not merely a suffering class, but one that was forced to
fight its oppression, one that was obliged to 'help itself'.[4] Thus says
Engels about the work in the new factory:

> It offers no field for mental activity, and claims just enough of his
> [the worker's] attention to keep him from thinking of anything
> else. And a sentence to such work, to work which takes his whole
> time for itself, leaving him scarcely time to eat and sleep, none
> for physical exercise in the open air, or the enjoyment of Nature,
> much less for mental activity, how can such a sentence help
> degrading a human being to the level of a brute? Once more the
> worker must choose, must either surrender himself to his fate,
> become a 'good workman', heed 'faithfully' the interest of the
> bourgeoisie, in which case he most certainly becomes a brute, or
> else he must rebel, fight for his manhood to the last, and this he
> can do only in the fight against the bourgeoisie. (4: 415–16)[5]

The entire book is focused on the emergence of this new class
and the historical significance of that emergence. Thus although
Engels set out to survey the conditions of the working class as a
whole, rather than confining himself to a particular industry as
many previous studies had, his book is nonetheless not *simply* such a
survey. Nor is *The Condition* merely a statement and systematisation
of the facts that Engels so carefully recorded. His conclusions went
far beyond the particular historical situation which provided the
factual basis for his study: his main conclusion was that the working
class is not simply capable of fighting its capitalist oppression but of
establishing the basis for a new society. 'The condition of the
working class is the real basis and point of departure of all social
movements of the present because it is the highest and most un-
concealed pinnacle of the social misery existing in our day.' This

allowed Engels to speak of the 'world-historical significance' of the transformation he studied. (4: 302)

The Condition is, above all, a general analysis of the development of industrial capitalism and the social impact of that development, the most important feature of which was the emergence of the modern labour movement. That is why Engels tells us that he does not intend to write a history of the industrial revolution but to conduct his study from the point of view of grasping the nature of the English working class:

> We have not, here and now, to deal with the history of this [the industrial] revolution, nor with its vast importance for the present and the future. Such a delineation must be reserved for a future, more comprehensive work. For the moment, we must limit ourselves to the little that is necessary for understanding the facts that follow, *for comprehending the present state of the English proletariat*. (emphasis added) (4: 307)

Engels's conclusions about the nature of the working class was arrived at on the basis of a most detailed and conscientious study of the conditions in which the working class was obliged to live. He not only drew on a wide range of literary sources (Peter Gaskell, John Wade, George Richardson Porter, Edward Baines, Andrew Ure, Thomas Carlyle, amongst others),[6] but he made full use of the official reports of the parliamentary commissioners, factory inspectors and statisticians. Reports from workers were obtained from the Chartist newspaper *The Northern Star*, which published regular articles and letters from workers, and Engels attended many workers' meetings. Last but not least Engels made extensive visits to working-class districts in Manchester ('the first manufacturing city of the world' [4: 355]) and surrounding towns, often accompanied by his companion, the young Irish woman, Mary Burns.[7] In this respect Engels's work remains a powerful refutation of the still-existing prejudice that Marxism is based on empty speculation and that Marxists are perforce hostile to empirical investigations.[8] This was the charge of the Young Hegelians who accused Marx and others of producing speculative constructs of world history.[9] The fact is that long before the appearance of 'empirical sociology', Marx and Engels engaged in a series of concrete social studies, of which *The Condition* is an outstanding early example.

What marks *The Condition* is its recognition that something unique was taking place in England in general and in the industrial towns of the north in particular, where work for his book was undertaken. The year before he wrote *The Condition* Engels had spoken thus about the profound developments occurring in England:

The century of revolution has to all appearances passed England by, causing little change. While on the Continent an entire old world was shattered, while a twenty-five year war cleared the air, in England everything remained calm, neither state nor church were in any way threatened. And yet since the middle of the last century England has experienced a greater upheaval than any other country – an upheaval which is all the more momentous the more quietly it is brought about, and it will therefore in all probability attain its goal more readily in practice than the political revolution in France or the philosophical revolution in Germany. The revolution in England is a social one and therefore more comprehensive and far-reaching than any other. There are no fields – however remote – of human knowledge and no conditions of life which have not contributed to it and which in turn have not been affected by it. (3: 469)

He makes a similar point in *The Condition*:

Sixty, eighty years ago, England was a country like every other, with small towns, few and simple industries, and a thin but *proportionally* large agricultural population. Today it is a country like *no* other, with a capital of two and a half million inhabitants; with vast manufacturing cities; with an industry that supplies the world, and produces almost everything by means of the most complex machinery; with an industrious, intelligent, dense population of which two thirds are employed in trade and commerce, and *composed of classes wholly different* [emphasis added]; forming, in fact, with other customs and other needs, a different nation from the England of those days. The industrial revolution is of the same importance for England as the political revolution for France, and the philosophical revolution for Germany; and the difference between England in 1760 and 1844 is at least as great as that between France under the *ancien regime* and during the revolution of July. (4: 320) [10]

In the series of articles that Engels contributed to *Vorwarts* in September–October 1844 he says:

The German, the nation of Christian spiritualism, experienced a philosophical revolution; the French, the nation of classical materialism and hence of politics, had to go through a political revolution; the English, a nation that is a mixture of German and French elements, who therefore embody both sides of the antithesis and are for that reason more universal than either of the two factors taken separately, were for that reason drawn into a more universal, a *social* revolution. (emphasis added)

The history of the English working classes begins in the second half of the eighteenth century with the invention of the steam engine and machines for spinning and weaving cotton. It is well known that these inventions gave the impetus to the genesis of an industrial revolution. The significance of this revolution in the history of the world is only now beginning to be understood. These momentous changes have occurred earlier and on a larger scale in England than elsewhere. The fact that these great changes sometimes took place without arousing much comment or publicity should not disguise their profound significance. In the circumstances it is only in England that the main social consequences of the Industrial revolution – the emergence of an industrial proletariat – can be satisfactorily studied in all its varied aspects.[11]

For Engels these fundamental changes were summed up in the notion of an 'industrial revolution'. He was not the first to employ such a term. In England it is one associated with the name of Arnold Toynbee (1852–83) whose posthumously-published *Lectures on the Industrial Revolution of the Eighteenth Century in England* (1884) seems to have been the first book to use the term in its title.[12] But despite the widespread belief to the contrary, Toynbee and his followers did not invent the term. Understandably, it originated with French writers in the 1820s and 1830s where a parallel between the technical changes then taking place in the major cotton manufacturing centres and the revolutions of 1789 and 1830 was drawn.[13] It was these references that Engels almost certainly had in mind when at the very opening of his book he spoke of the 'industrial revolution' as being something 'well known' (4: 307). But if Engels was not the first to deploy the term, he was the first to invest it 'with the full force of a revolutionary event'.[14] Whereas others 'knew' that an industrial revolution was under way, Engels was the first to grasp its true, world-historical, significance, that is, its profound social meaning.

Engels's conception of the industrial revolution has been subject to a variety of attacks.[15] In the first place the notion of an 'industrial revolution' has been derided as a piece of German Romanticism, a product of the baleful influence exercised over him by Hegel and Moses Hess in particular. In the second place, the whole idea of an industrial revolution ever having taken place has been increasingly questioned by economic historians. Here the object of criticism is not simply Engels but a long line of historians that would include Toynbee, the Hammonds, Paul Mantoux and others. We will look at these two lines of criticism in turn. It was Engels's supposed Romanticism, so the story goes, that allowed him to depict the industrial revolution as a 'transcendent historical process', to be set side by side with other sorts of revolution in France and Germany, and carrying inevitable implications for the future. This conception was clearly 'a child of Romanticism'.[16] In similar vein, Engels is accused of presenting the industrial revolution as a 'social catastrophe', something that destroyed a state of pre-lapsarian bliss. There are certainly passages in *The Condition*, which, if torn out of context, might give rise to such an impression. Thus:

> Before the introduction of machinery, the spinning and weaving of raw materials was carried on in the working man's home. Wife and daughter spun the yarn that the father wove or that they sold, if he did not work it up himself. These weaver families lived in the country in the neighbourhood of the towns, and could get on fairly well with their wages, because the home market was almost the only one, and the crushing power of competition that came later, with the conquest of foreign markets and the extension of trade, did not yet press upon wages. (4: 307–8)

And a little further on:

> So the workers vegetated throughout a passably comfortable existence, leading a righteous and peaceful life in all piety and probity; and their material position was far better than that of their successors. They did not need to overwork; they did no more than they chose to do, and yet earned what they needed ... They were, for the most part, strong, well-built people, in whose physique little or no difference from that of their peasant neighbours was discoverable. (4: 308)

But this is far from all that Engels has to say about conditions in pre-industrial England. For on the very next page we find:

> But intellectually they were dead; lived only for their petty, private interest, for their looms and gardens, and knew nothing of the mighty movement which, beyond their horizon, was sweeping through mankind. They were comfortable in their silent vegetation, and but for the industrial revolution would never have emerged from this existence, which, cosily romantic though it was, was nevertheless not worthy of human beings; they were merely toiling machines in the service of the few aristocrats who had guided history down to that time. The industrial revolution has simply carried this out to its logical end by making the workers machines pure and simple, taking from them the last trace of independent activity, and so forcing them to think and demand a position worthy of men. As in France politics, so in England manufacture and the movement of civil society in general drew into the world of history the last classes which had remained

sunk in apathetic indifference to the universal interests of mankind. (4: 309)[17]

Comparing the lot of the modern worker, living under conditions of 'hypocritical slavery', with the serf, Engels says:

> But the hypocritical disguised slavery recognises the right to freedom, at least in outward form; bows before a freedom-loving public opinion, and herein lies the historic progress as compared with the old servitude, that the *principle* of freedom is affirmed, and the oppressed will one day see to it that the principle is carried out. (4: 474)

Or again:

> In the patriarchal relation that deceitfully concealed the slavery of the workers, he had to remain spiritually dead, entirely unknowing of his own interests and a mere private, isolated being. Only when the worker became estranged from his master did matter change. Only then did it become manifest that he was connected with his employer solely through the cash nexus. Then the ostensible bond of affection between them proved unable to bear the slightest test and fell entirely away. And it was only then that the worker began to recognise his position in this relationship and to develop independently. Only now did he cease to be the slave of the middle classes in his thoughts, feelings and acts of will.

In other words, the industrial revolution was a profoundly *contradictory* event: it brought misery and degradation for the working class but, simultaneously, through the creation of just such a class, it laid the basis for a newer, truly human form of society. Criticising the Owenites for their attitude to the working class, he says of such socialists:

> While bemoaning the demoralisation of the lower classes, they are blind to *the element of progress in the dissolution of the old social order* [emphasis added], and refuse to acknowledge that the corruption wrought by private interests and hypocrisy in the property-holding class is much greater. *They acknowledge no historic development* [emphasis added] and wish to place the nation in a state of Communism at once, overnight, not by the unavoidable march of its political development up to the point at which this transition becomes both possible and necessary. They understand, it is true, why the working-man is resentful against the bourgeois, but regard as unfruitful this class hatred, which is after all, the

only moral incentive by which the worker can be brought nearer the goal. (4: 525)

Thomas Carlyle is the man most often accused of providing Engels with his Romantic view of the industrial revolution.[18] There is no doubt that Engels greatly admired Carlyle's work.[19] Carlyle had 'sounded the social disorder more deeply than any other English bourgeois' (4: 578); his *Past and Present* was 'the only one which strikes a human chord, presents human relations and shows traces of a human point of view' (3: 444). Carlyle had condemned the British ruling class for having plunged the English people into unprecedented impoverishment, degradation and moral evil. And Engels found Carlyle's criticisms of capitalism all the more valuable because they were admissions wrung from a member of the ruling class. Engels also quotes with approval Carlyle's exposure of bourgeois democracy: 'The notion that a man's liberty consists in giving his vote at election-hustings and saying, "Behold, now I too have my twenty-thousandth part of a Talker in our National Palaver; will not the gods be good to me?" – is one of the pleasantest.'

But to imply that this involved an uncritical acceptance of Carlyle's viewpoint is patently absurd. For Carlyle's class standpoint made it impossible for him to take a scientific approach to the problems of doing away with the evils he had so eloquently and passionately described. Carlyle saw the evils produced by the development of capitalism as rooted not in capitalism itself but in atheism and the self-seeking supposedly connected with it. Accepting that there can be no return to the past, he has visions of a new religion based on pantheism and the cult of labour, a position that Engels rejects as a reactionary utopia. Whereas according to Carlyle, society must be saved from the social evils stemming from capitalist civilisation by a 'true aristocracy', for Engels it is in the working class that 'the strength and the capacity of development of the nation' reposes (4: 529). Only the workers 'are really respectable, for all their roughness and for all their moral degradation. It is from them that England's salvation will come, they still comprise flexible material; they have no education, but no prejudices either, they still have a future (3: 445–6).[20] It is on this basis that Engels condemns the reactionary conception of 'heroes' and 'the mob' which Carlyle sought to justify on the basis of the failure of democracy.

As we have stressed, the fundamental point for Engels about the industrial revolution was that its 'mightiest result' (4: 320) was the creation of a new class, the working class, a class that was forced to fight against its conditions of oppression. In other words for him this was a *social* revolution, not something to be reduced to narrowly technical matters such as the inventions that occurred in this period, important though these were. It is from this angle that

Engels sees the importance of the introduction of the spinning jenny: 'While the industrial proletariat was thus developing with the first very imperfect machine, the same machine gave rise to the agricultural proletariat' (4: 311). Or again, 'Having already seen what a transformation in the social condition of the lower classes a single such clumsy machine as the jenny has wrought, there is no cause for surprise as to that which a complete and interdependent system of finely adjusted machinery has brought about ...' (4: 312–13).

It is this aspect of the industrial revolution – as something marking a fundamental change in British economic and social structure – that has been subject to increasing attack over the recent past. The attack has gained such ground that some historians are now obliged to talk in terms of the need to 'rehabilitate' the industrial revolution.[21] This is no doubt part of the more general claim that British history has been free of sharp turning points, free of violent interruptions, a history characterised by Fabian gradualness. In this respect the attack is not confined to Engels but is directed at a long line of economic and social historians from Arnold Toynbee onwards.[22] Although gaining pace in recent years, the repudiation of the idea of an industrial revolution marking a unique turning point in British history was first evidenced in the 1920s and 1930s in the work of people such as Clapham, Redford and Ashton. These writers stressed the long tap-roots of industrialisation, its unevenness and incompleteness. Their work marked a turn away from the social character of the great changes taking place from the middle of the eighteenth century onwards in favour of a study of the technical changes occurring in industry which went hand-in-hand with a concentration on 'growth rates'. But even then, the majority of historians retained the idea that something that could properly be called an 'industrial revolution' had taken place.[23]

In this respect recent work has taken a step forward, or more accurately a step backwards, in that the very idea of the existence of an industrial revolution in Britain is increasingly rejected, or where the term is accepted it is drained of its social content.[24] Much of this research – the 'new economic history' – has concentrated on statistical work which seeks to show, for instance, that the rate of growth during the period of the industrial revolution was much slower than had previously been thought, and that much of the economy remained unaffected by the technical changes that were taking place in the cotton textile industry. Some writers have laid great stress on the fact that recent estimates of national income over the period concerned show far slower rates of growth than the earlier estimates of Deane and Cole. According to the latest calculations growth was particularly slow in the last four decades of the eighteenth century. The problem here is not so much the fragile data on which these 'estimates' are made but the meaning to be attached to them. For what is crucial is not the quantitative rate of growth of national income but the *qualitative* transformation of social relations in Britain in the century up to 1850. This raises important theoretical problems. No economic system, least of all the capitalist economy, can be understood as a series of 'sectors' which stand side-by-side in some passive relationship. It is the *interaction* of its various sectors that determines the real dynamic of an economy. Thus in the case of the world economy: its momentum is determined by the real, changing relationships between its various national components. Its movement cannot be understood by resort to simple arithmetical entities – for instance average growth rates, even average growth rates of the manufacturing sector. Such statistics can disclose little about the real forces which either impel forward or retard its development. Naturally no economic historian is unaware of the fact that there were marked disparities in the growth rates of the different sectors of the economy both during the pre-industrial period and then during the industrial revolution itself. But the matter is not simply one of quantities, as many seem to believe.[25]

The manner in which Trotsky set out to grasp the peculiarities of Russia's economic development in the period before 1917 is here instructive from the point of view of method. Could, for example, the dynamic of economic relations in pre-1917 Russia be understood from the smallness of the working class as a proportion of the total population? This sort of question, Trotsky makes clear, can only be approached concretely, from the standpoint of the real interrelations within the economy – as they had arisen historically. The working class, although a tiny proportion of a population comprising largely peasants, was a relatively new phenomenon. Thanks to Russia's belated economic development, because industrialisation took place on the basis of techniques and forms of organisation already developed in the west, the working class was concentrated in some of the most advanced factories in Europe. This gave it a specific weight which no simple averaging of the population could disclose; on the contrary, such averaging could lead only to the conclusion that the working class was a relatively powerless class.

Thus Trotsky says:

But it is just in the sphere of economy ... that the law of combined development most forcibly emerges. At the same time that peasant land-cultivation as a whole remained, right up to the revolution, at the level of the seventeenth century, Russian industry in its technique and capitalist structure stood at the level of the advanced countries, and in certain respects even outstripped them. Small enterprises, involving less than 100 workers, employed in the United States in 1914, 35 per cent of the total industrial workers, but in Russia only 17.8 per cent.[26]

The same methodological questions that are involved in grasping the nature and dynamic of the industrial revolution in Britain arose in the dispute in the 1920s about whether socialism in a single country, Russia, was feasible. It was Bukharin who argued that because the correlation between the working class and the peasantry in the USSR corresponded to the 'average' figure for the world economy, this meant that the conditions for building socialism in the Soviet Union were no less or no more favourable than anywhere else. Replying to Bukharin's 'scholastic casuistry' Trotsky made the following remark (if 'industrial revolution' is substituted for 'world revolution' and 'national revolution', Trotsky's point has more than a little relevance for the present discussion):

In the first place it is quite probable that the correlation of forces between the proletariat and the peasantry on the world scale is not very much different from the correlation within the USSR. But the world revolution is not accomplished in accordance with the method of the arithmetic mean, and, incidentally, neither is the national revolution. Thus the October Revolution occurred and entrenched itself first in proletarian Petrograd, instead of choosing such a region where the correlation between the workers and peasants would correspond to the average for the whole of Russia. After Petrograd and later Moscow had created the revolutionary government and the revolutionary army, they had to overthrow the bourgeoisie in the outlying country, in the course of several years; and only as a result of this process, called revolution, was there established within the boundaries of the USSR the present correlation between the proletariat and the peasantry. The revolution does not occur in accordance with the method of the arithmetic mean. It can begin in a less favourable sector, but until it entrenches itself in the decisive sectors of both the national and the world frontiers, it is impermissible to speak about its complete victory.[27]

A general issue is involved in this discussion about recent trends in economic history, namely the tendency to separate out narrowly 'economic' question from wider social processes. According to an earlier comment by one writer:

... it is now unusual for economic historians in Britain to refer in their specialist or their general writing to historical categories or types of societies, and any discussion of change, of early industrialisation, for instance, is set in generalised terms relating to 'the industrial revolution,' or to the period of 'take off,' without reference to the broader context of society in which these events occurred. There has come about a narrowing of interest from society at large to the more limited problems of economic growth and change. Social questions are nearly always considered separately from economic development; political matters are left entirely alone.[28]

It is one of the contentions of the 'new economic history' that the development of the industrial sector during the 'industrial revolution' was far less rapid than has hitherto been thought. But here again two matters arise. In the first place, it must again be stressed that simple averages cannot disclose the real relationship of forces at work. Landes makes a telling point which is worth quoting at length:

In sum one must not mistake the appearance for the reality. The census returns and other numbers [are] ... without the virtue of wholeness to compensate for their lifelessness ... numbers merely describe the surface of ... society and even then in terms that define away change by using categories of unchanging nomenclature. Beneath this surface, the vital organs were transformed and though they weighed but a fraction of the total ... it was they that determined the metabolism of the entire system. We have seen that, in so far as small-scale enterprise continued to flourish, it did so largely because of demand derived from the growth of concentrated manufacture: the demand of the large producers themselves; of their employees; and of the urban agglomerations that grew up around them. But not only small industry was tied in this way to the modern sector. Agriculture, trade, banking – all came increasingly to depend on the needs, the products, the bills of exchange, the investments of Lancashire, the Midlands, and the other nodes of British factory industry.[29]

The fact is that it was a qualitative breakthrough in one branch of textiles – cotton spinning – that was decisive.[30] And we stress 'qualitative' because the 'breakthrough' was not simply a quantitative matter. It was the development of the *factory system*, the development of *industrial capitalism* in that sphere that is the vital issue. In other words it was not merely, or primarily, changes in the techniques of production that led to a development of the productive forces during the period of the industrial revolution, but a transformation of the social relations of production, albeit initially in one sector.

Second, and just as important: we can say that while the 'breakthrough' was made in cotton textiles, such a development would have been impossible without the fundamental changes that took place in English agriculture in the three hundred years, 1500–1800. Unless the relationship between the industrial and agricultural sectors is grasped then the origins of the industrial revolution in England will be lost. In the last resort it will be impossible to answer the question, why was it that that 'primitive machine' (Engels) introduced into one sector of one branch of production (textiles) could set in motion such a profound social transformation of England? Clearly not because of the *material* qualities of the machine *per se* but because the social conditions were ripe in England in a way that they were not elsewhere. (We will return shortly to this question of the 'natural' and the 'social'.) And in grasping this 'ripeness', the revolution brought about in agriculture holds the key.

As Saville puts it:

> Above all, the experience of Britain in respect of the transformation of her social structure prior to industrialisation has not been paralleled in the history of any other industrialising society. Nowhere save in Britain was the peasantry virtually eliminated *before* the acceleration of economic growth that is associated with the development of industrial capitalism, and of the many special features of early industrialisation in Britain none is more striking than the pressure of a rapidly growing proletariat in the countryside.[31]

The major theme of this chapter has been the defence of the notion of the industrial revolution as above all a *social phenomenon*, as against those who see the revolution (assuming they think that such a term has any validity) in narrowly technical terms. This issue has wider implications than merely an appreciation of the character of the industrial revolution. It is to these wider implications that we briefly turn. For those who wish to see in the industrial revolution simply the application of new inventions to the productive process, who wish to concentrate their attention on increases in labour productivity and 'growth rates', are in fact guilty of confusing the 'technical' with the 'social', of fetishising science.[32]

It was the so-called 'scientific and technological revolution' that supposedly occurred after 1945 that led many to talk about the 'transformation' of capitalism, and some to speak in terms of a 'new' industrial revolution.[33] Thus the once fashionable notion of 'industrial society' is based on claims that the imperatives of technical change in the post-war world have made it essential for large corporations to plan their economic growth over long periods of time, ignoring the principles of profit maximisation. The claim was that advances in technology have made the planning and the marketing of goods and services, as well as their production by means of data-processing systems, a necessary component of management. The conclusion drawn by Galbraith and others was that power now lies in the hands of a 'technostructure', a stratum engendered by the 'technological and scientific revolution' and one that shuns the traditional capitalist mentality, a social group that seeks optimal profit in a manner that attenuates or even eliminates the traditional conflict between capital and labour. In the 'new world order' (in fact it is a world of chaos) such ideas seem positively antediluvian when compared with what Engels wrote 150 years ago.[34]

But it is not simply the apologists for capitalism who have contended that, thanks to the development of science and technology, there has been a decisive change in contemporary capitalism. It is here that important questions about the degeneration of Marxism in the present century must be addressed. The enormous damage done to the theoretical heritage of Marxism by its Stalinist perversion is now widely recognised. It was Stalinism that distorted historical materialism almost beyond recognition when it presented history as a series of fixed stages through which each society would automatically progress. Relations of production would adjust semi-automatically to the level attained in the ever-upward progress of the productive forces. And these forces of production were in turn interpreted narrowly to mean productive techniques, or the implements of labour or natural forces brought under control by technology: with the 'working class' sometimes 'added on' as one of the productive forces. These mechanical conceptions reached their nadir with the writings of Stalin – or rather the writings that were issued in his name. But it is clear that this degeneration was by no means confined to those under the direct influence of Stalinism. For example, amongst those who saw a new industrial revolution having taken place in the post-1945 period was Ernest Mandel – in his case this was the 'third industrial revolution' known to history. For Mandel this latest industrial revolution was based on the emergence of a series of new, 'high tech' industries alongside the growing involvement of the state in the regulation of the economy. He coined the phrase 'neo-capitalism' to describe this new and distinct state in the evolution of capitalism. Writing in the 1960s he had the following to say:

> With the 1940s appeared the warning signs of a third industrial revolution. The first industrial revolution had been based on the steam engine, the second on the electric motor and the combustion engine. The third industrial revolution is based on the release of nuclear energy and the use of electronic machinery.[35]

It is this phrase 'based on' that is misleading. The industrial revolution was *not* 'based on the steam engine'. Certainly the industrial revolution involved the application of steam power to productive processes, but, as we have argued, such applications were possible only because of the transformation of social relations in agriculture that preceded the industrial revolution. The crux of the matter is that the introduction of machinery in the late eighteenth and early nineteenth centuries brought a new class into existence. It seems clear that, like many others, Mandel has managed to drain his conception of 'industrial revolution' of its social, class content. His second and third 'industrial revolutions' were in no real sense industrial revolutions for, unlike the first, they singularly failed to bring new classes and new class relations into being. In this vital respect, then, the 'first' industrial revolution was the only one that Britain has experienced. In one respect at least Mandel is consistent. For if indeed the post-war period has witnessed a new industrial revolution, then this must mark a new stage in the development of capitalism – what Mandel calls 'neo-capitalism':

> I do not care very much for the term 'neo-capitalism' which is ambiguous, to say the least. Nevertheless I am quite convinced that starting either with the great depression of 1929–32 or with the second world war, capitalism entered into a third stage of its development, *which is as different from monopoly capitalism or imperialism as described by Lenin, Hilferding and others as monopoly capitalism was different from classical laissez faire capitalism* [emphasis added]. We have to give this child a name; all other names proposed seem even less acceptable than 'neo-capitalism'. 'State monopoly capitalism', the term used in the Soviet Union and the 'official' communist parties, is very misleading because it implies a degree of independence of the state which, to my mind, does not at all correspond to present-day reality. On the contrary, I would say that today the state is a much more direct instrument for guaranteeing monopoly surplus profit to the strongest private monopolies than it ever was in the past. The German *Spaetkapitalismus* seems interesting, but simply indicates a time sequence and is difficult to translate into several languages.[36]

Now if the 'industrial revolution' is narrowed down to a technical phenomenon – as I believe is the case with writers such as Mandel – it is impossible to understand the development of consciousness that took place in the century following 1750. For one outstanding feature of the industrial revolution was that it not only saw the emergence of a new class, the working class, but witnessed a profound development in the consciousness of this class.

In *The Condition* Engels outlines the situation of the worker and what it means for his fight against the capitalist:

> The worker is the passive subject of all possible combination of circumstances and can count himself fortunate when he has saved his life even for a short time; and his character and way of living are naturally shaped by these conditions. Either he seeks to keep his head above water in this whirlpool, to rescue his manhood, and this he can do solely in rebellion against the class which

plunders him so mercilessly and then abandons him to his fate ... or he gives up the struggle against his fate as hopeless. (4: 413)

Or later:

It must be admitted, even if I had not proved it so often in detail, that the English workers cannot feel happy in this condition; that theirs is not a state in which a man or a whole class of men can think, feel and live as human beings. The worker must therefore strive to escape from this brutalising condition, to secure for themselves a better, more human position; and this they cannot do without attacking the interest of the bourgeoisie which consists in exploiting them. But the bourgeoisie defends its interests with all the power placed at its disposal by the wealth and the might of the State. In proportion as the working-man determines to alter the present state of things, the bourgeois becomes his avowed enemy. (4: 501)

Commenting on passages such as these Steven Marcus says that their interest lies in the fact that they express the idea that the creation of a working-class or labour movement will have to be the activity of the working class itself.

It represents one of the earliest acknowledgements by a socialist writer of any theoretical standing of this critical historical circumstance, and distinguishes in advance the kind of socialism that Marx and Engels were to develop theoretically from the socialism of their immediate predecessors, the Owenites, Saint-Simonians, and Fourierists and the socialists in Germany.[37]

Here lies the significance of Lenin's earlier insistence that Engels grasped the fact that the working class was no helpless object, the mere plaything of history, but that its very condition forced it to 'help itself'. Engels traces the general path of this development of working-class consciousness. Starting in some cases with crime it grows through machine-breaking, in which the working class 'first manifested opposition to the bourgeoisie' (4: 503), through trade unionism, finally to reach Chartism.[38]

One of the legacies of the distortion of Marxism for which Stalinism was principally responsible was the mechanical separation between the struggle of the working class and revolutionary class consciousness. It was Karl Kautsky who rightly said that revolutionary class consciousness was brought into the movement 'from the outside', a proposition which Lenin strongly supported against those (the 'economists') who conceived of revolutionary class consciousness developing in a purely spontaneous manner. But at the same time Lenin recognised that the working class tended to gravitate towards such a revolutionary consciousness, Marxism, if only because Marxism best explained its historical and objective situation.

In this regard, Engels's comments on the relationship of Chartism to socialist theory are of considerable contemporary significance:

> Hence it is evident that the working-men's movement is divided into two sections, the Chartists and the Socialists. The Chartists are theoretically the more backward, the less developed, but they are genuine proletarians all over, the representatives of their class. The Socialists are more far-seeing, propose practical remedies against distress, but, proceeding originally from the bourgeoisie, are for this reason unable to amalgamate completely with the working class. The union of Socialism with Chartism ... will be the next step, and has already begun. Then only, when this has been achieved, will the working class be the true intellectual leader of England. Meanwhile, political and social development will proceed, and will foster this new party, this new departure of Chartism. (4: 526–7)[39]

This was written some 150 years ago. Today the working class in Britain stands in need of a 'new party'; the leaders of its traditional party, the Labour Party, have now turned their back explicitly on anything to do with socialism. Clause Four of the Labour Party constitution has been abandoned and Tony Blair and company make no secret of their aim to transform the Labour Party into a version of the US Democratic Party, that is an openly bourgeoisie party. The sort of party that is needed is one that follows Engels's conception: not one that stands apart from the working class, preaching to it from high up, but one that is an integral part of its daily struggles.

In this respect, Engels's comments are as fresh today as the day they were written. According to one writer: 'Engels's book remains today, as it was in 1845, by far the best single book on the working class of the period.'[40] No doubt the research of the last 150 years has added to our knowledge of the working class. But in its theoretical conceptions, in its grasp of the period and its consequences, in its look into the future, *The Condition* remains unsurpassed. It was a truly revolutionary book. Not only did it assist Marx to become 'a Marxist' but it represented a vital stage in the elaboration of historical materialism. We have drawn attention to the disastrous and stultifying impact which Stalinism had on Marxism. Engels's *The Condition* has nothing whatsoever in common with the crude, mechanical distortions that for decades passed as Marxism in many intellectual circles. In the task of re-appropriating the heritage of Marxism, and in the task of developing it creatively in line with today's requirements: the book of the 24-year-old Engels will surely occupy a central place.

Notes

1 I should like to thank Terry Brotherstone for some helpful comments on an earlier draft.

2 27: 313–14.

3 In the Preface to the English edition (1892), he had the following to say about this earlier position: 'Thus great stress is laid on the dictum that Communism is not a mere party doctrine of the working class, but a theory encompassing the emancipation of society at large, including the capitalist class, from its present narrow conditions. This is true enough in the abstract, but absolutely useless, and sometimes worse, in practice. So long as the wealthy classes not only do not feel the want of any emancipation, but strenuously oppose the self-emancipation of the working class, so long the social revolution will have to be prepared and fought out by the working class alone' (27: 261).

4 This should not lead us to ignore the book as a purely historical piece of work. According to one writer, even today, as an empirical account of the working class and its conditions, it stands unrivalled. See Steven Marcus, *Engels, Manchester and the Working Class*, Weidenfeld and Nicolson, 1974.

5 This was Lenin's estimation: 'Even before Engels, many people had described the sufferings of the proletariat, and had pointed to the necessity of helping it. Engels was the first to say that the proletariat is not only a suffering class; that it is, in fact, the disgraceful economic conditions of the proletariat that drives it irresistibly forward and compels it to fight for its ultimate emancipation. And the fighting proletariat *will help itself*' (*LCW* 4: 22). The revolutionary role of the working class is a theme strongly present in *The Holy Family*, which was published the year prior to *The Condition*. Marx and Engels speak there of 'the world historic role of the proletariat' which 'executes the sentence that private property pronounces on itself' (4: 36).

6 None of these writers shared Engels's conception that an industrial and social revolution was under way in England, though Gaskell came close when he spoke of 'one of the most striking revolutions ever produced in the moral and social condition of a moiety of a great nation that which has been consequent to the application of steam to machinery'. Peter Gaskell, *The Manufacturing Population of England*, quoted in D. C. Coleman, *Myth, History and the Industrial Revolution*, The Hambledon Press, 1992, p. 6. For an account of the sources used by Engels, see W. O. Henderson, *The Life of Friedrich Engels*, (2 vols, Frank Cass, 1976, vol. 1, Chapter 2).

7 Explaining the significance of the position of Manchester, Engels says: 'Hence because Manchester is the classic type of a modern manufacturing town, and because I know it as intimately as my own native town, more intimately than most of its residents know it, we shall make a longer stay here.' (4: 345)

8 The 'Marxist' defence of this position found its most absurd expression in the work of Louis Althusser. Cf. Lenin's remarks about Marx's *Capital*: 'He took one of the economic formations of society – the system of commodity production – *and on the basis of a vast mass of data* [emphasis added] which he studied for no less that twenty-five years. gave a most detailed analysis of the laws governing the functioning of this formation and its development' (*LCW* 1, p. 141).

9 In the Preface to the German edition (1845), Engels accuses German communism and socialism of having started from theoretical premises alone and of knowing too little of the real world and this 'bad reality' (4: 303). For Marx's and Engels's attitude to the Young Hegelians see *The Holy Family*, their first joint work and published before *The Condition*.

10 At least some of the leading socialists came to recognise the social implications of the momentous changes that had taken place in England. Thus the Owenite James Hole could write in 1851: 'Class stands opposed to class, and so accustomed have men become to pursue their own isolated interests apart from a regardless of that of others, that it has become an acknowledged maxim, that when a man pursues his own interests alone he is most benefiting society – a maxim ... which would justify every crime and folly ... The principle of supply and demand has been extended from commodities to men. These have obtained more liberty, but less bread. They find that in parting with the thraldom of Feudalism they have taken on that of Capital; that slavery has ceased in name but survived in fact.' James Hole, *Lectures on Social Science*, quoted in Asa Briggs, *Victorian Cities*, Penguin, 1963, p. 140.

11 Cf. Marx: 'Great Britain, of all the other countries, has seen developed on the greatest scale, the despotism of Capital and the slavery of Labour. In no other country have the intermediate stations between the millionaire commanding whole industrial armies and the wage-slave living from hand to mouth so gradually been swept away from the soil. There exist here no longer, as in continental countries, large classes of peasants and artisans almost equally dependent on their own property and their own labour. A complete divorce of property from labour has been effected in Great Britain. In no other country, therefore has the war between the two classes that constitute modern society assumed so colossal dimensions and features so distinct and palpable.' Marx, letter to the Labour Parliament, 9 March 1854.

12 For a survey of the historiography of the industrial revolution from Toynbee onwards, see D. Cannadine, 'The Past and the Present in the English Industrial Revolution, 1880–1980', *Past and Present*, 103, 1984, pp. 149–58. Cannadine suggests that the interpretation of the industrial revolution has passed through four distinct phases. Initially its social consequences were stressed, then it was examined as an example of a series of cyclical fluctuations, then as a case of 'economic growth', and finally in terms of the fashionable 'limits to growth' theory.

13 A. Bezanson, 'The Early Use of the Term Industrial Revolution', *Quarterly Journal of Economics*, 36, 1922, pp. 342–9.

14 Gertrude Himmelfarb, *The Idea of Poverty*, 1984, p. 282, quoted in D. C. Coleman, *Myth*, p. 3.

15 We leave aside the cruder attacks that claim that Engels deliberately misused his sources to paint an unnecessarily grim picture of the industrial revolution. The most notorious of such attacks was that of Chaloner and Henderson in their edition of *The Condition*. For a reply to this sort of attack, see E. J. Hobsbawm, 'The Dark Satanic Mills', in Hobsbawm's *Labouring Men: Studies in the History of Labour*, Weidenfeld and Nicolson, 1964, pp. 105–119.

16 D. C. Coleman, *Myth*, p. 7. How Engels's notion of the industrial revolution can be characterised as 'transcendent' when it is sustained with such a mass of concrete empirical material is difficult to comprehend.

17 'The Industrial revolution ... [made] the workers machines pure and simple, taking from them the last trace of independent activity, and so forcing them to think and demand a position worthy of men. As in France politics, so in England manufacture and the movement of civil society in general drew into the whirl of history the last classes which had remained sunk in apathetic indifference to the universal interests of mankind' (4: 309). It is in this spirit that Engels condemns any idea that there can be a return to some pre-industrial state, as Disraeli, Lord Ashley and other members of Young England were at the time proposing. Such an object was quite 'unobtainable' says Engels, 'ridiculous', 'a satire upon all historical development' (4: 578).

18 'Among Engels's English language sources one provided a close link with the world of German Romanticism, itself a vital spring of Engels's historical argument. Thomas Carlyle was himself, of course, greatly influenced by Romanticism ... Carlyle's thunderous rhetorical assault upon the "condition of England" in *Past and Present* appealed to Engels's revolutionary sentiments as well as seeming to offer support for the evidence of his own eyes on his arrival in England in November 1842.' Coleman, *Myth*, pp. 6–7.

19 It was at the conclusion of his review of Carlyle's *Past and Present* that Engels declared that he must carry out a more detailed examination of the condition of England: 'The condition of England is of immense importance for history and for all other countries; for as regard social matters England is of course far in advance of all other countries' (3: 468). This was a striking advance on Engels's contention at the end of 1842, when he considered England to be up to its ears in mediaeval backwardness.

20 'It is the working class that has put forward, through its social leaders, the Socialists, the task of destroying capitalism. And whatever weaknesses the Socialists might have (an inclination towards a narrow empiricism and practicalism) they are the only party in England which has a future ... Democracy, Chartism must soon be victorious and then

the mass of English workers will have the choice only between starvation and socialism' (3: 467). Engels's appreciation of the position of the working class measures the extent to which he and Marx had finished with the Young Hegelians. Bruno Bauer, for example, thought the masses, far from being a liberating force, were driven by ignorance and passion. Enslaved by the tyranny of 'the practical', by the narrow struggle to improve their lot, they were sunk in preoccupations with their material interests. For a trenchant critique of the revival of similar ideas in the recent past, see Ellen Meiksins Wood, *The Retreat from Class: a New 'True' Socialism*, Verso, 1986.

21 See Maxine Berg and Pat Hudson, 'Rehabilitating the Industrial Revolution' *Economic History Review*, XLV, 1992, pp. 24–50.

22 The industrial revolution has always been a matter for intense ideological debate. It is no accident that for much of the Cold War the apologists for capitalism sought to show that capitalist industrialisation was not inconsistent with rising living standards.. While the matter cannot be entered into fully here, it should be noted that neither Engels nor Marx ever held that the development of capitalism would bring with it an inevitable and irreversible 'immiseration' for the working class, nor that *all* workers had been plunged into poverty as a result of capitalist industrialisation (see, for example, 4: 372–3). In any case, crucially, Engels did not believe that revolution would occur because of the tendency to absolute impoverishment, but because of the tendency to social polarisation (4: 580). In this sense much of the heated controversy about the standard of living of the working class during the period of the industrial revolution was perhaps somewhat misplaced. For a recent survey of where that controversy has now reached, see John Rule, *The Labouring Classes in Early Industrial England, 1750–1850*, Longman, 1986.

23 This was not universally true, as the following statement written in 1927 indicates: 'When, on looking back, we find that the revolution has been going on for two centuries, and had been in preparation for two centuries before that, when we find that both in its causes and consequences it affects the lot of that three-quarters of the human race who are still farmers and peasants as profoundly as it does that of the industrial worker, we may begin to doubt whether the term ... has not by this time served its term.' George Unwin 'Some Economic Factors in General History', quoted in M. W. Flinn, *Origins of the Industrial Revolution*, Longman, 1966, p. 5.

24 The other side of the coin is that the idea of 'industrial revolution' has been greatly expanded. According to which economic historian you consult, you can find 'industrial revolutions' in the Bronze Age, the thirteenth century, the fifteenth century, the period 1540–1640, the late nineteenth and early twentieth centuries. Thus Professor Carus-Wilson saw the mechanisation of the process of fulling in the thirteenth century as constituting an industrial revolution; Nef saw an

industrial revolution in the century after 1540 as taking place in the coal industry which brought with it technical changes and the growth of large-scale industry. And this is only England! Germany and Japan in the late nineteenth centuries have their advocates. Walt Rostow claimed to discern no fewer than four industrial revolutions: the first in the period after 1780, associated with the textile industry; the second based on the railway boom of the 1830s; a third based on the steel, machine tools and motor vehicles of the late nineteenth and early twentieth centuries; and a fourth, still under way, based on electronics and developments in biology. What most of these conceptions share is a concentration on the narrow question of changes in the techniques of production. In any event, so wide is the use of the concept 'industrial revolution' that it loses all meaning.

25 See, for example, N. F. R. Crafts, 'The New Economic History and the Industrial Revolution', in Peter Mathias and John A. Davies, *The First Industrial Revolutions*, 1990. Crafts, a leading figure in the 'new economic history' school, accepts that there was something called an 'industrial revolution' in Britain. But his understanding of it is far different from that of Engels. He recognises that there was a pronounced structural change in the British economy with resources moving away from agriculture to industry, although, according to his calculations, this did not involve rapid changes in productivity in the latter sector. 'The "industrial revolution" consisted much more in getting a lot of workers into industry than of achieving very high productivity from them once there. It is Britain's agricultural productivity, release of labour from agriculture and triumph in cotton textile exports which emerge as truly remarkable.' Here again, the changes in agriculture that made such gains in *per capita* output possible were of a *social* character, involving as they did the triumph of capitalist relations in the countryside, a point emphasised below.

26 L. D. Trotsky, *History of the Russian Revolution*, Anchor Foundation, 1980, p. 1. The whole of Chapter 1, 'Peculiarities of Russia's Development', deals with this problem.

27 L. D. Trotsky, *The Third International After Lenin*, New Park Publications, 1974, p. 46. Trotsky suggested that this argument of Bukharin be included in a textbook on dialectics as an example of purely scholastic thinking.

28 J. Saville, 'Primitive Accumulation and Early Industrialisation in Britain', *Socialist Register*, 1969, p. 248. It is little wonder that one of our most prominent economic historians, R. M. Hartwell, admitted some years ago that the considerable recent empirical work 'has added little to our understanding of the industrial revolution'. R. Hartwell, 'The Causes of the Industrial revolution: An Essay in Methodology', quoted in Saville, 'Primitive Accumulation', p. 249.

29 David Landes, *The Unbound Prometheus: Technological Change and Industrial Development in Western Europe from 1750 to the Present*, Cambridge Uni-

versity Press, 1969, p. 122. For the significance of these remarks, see Berg and Hudson, 'Rehabilitating the Industrial Revolution'. The position of Landes is in sharp contrast to those who, on the basis that as late as 1850 many handicraft industries survived, located in small workshops, maintain that patterns of employment remained dominated by traditional craftsmen, labourers and domestic servants, that there was only a slow diffusion of steam power, and that we cannot properly speak of an 'industrial revolution'. In so doing they simply reveal the narrowness of their conception. See A. E. Musson, *The Growth of British Industry*, Batsford, 1978. See Cannadine, 'The Past and the Present in the English Industrial Revolution'.

30 Here again, those who abstract from the *social* content of the industrial revolution are able to argue that the experience of industrial Lancashire was atypical and that it was in fact the mercantile and consumer-dominated Home Counties that provided the main sources and stimulus to economic growth. This misses the point that the industrial revolution cannot be reduced to that of 'economic growth' either slow or rapid. It was the new factory system, with Manchester at its heart, that created the modern working class, and this is the decisive issue here.

31 Saville, 'Primitive Accumulation', p. 250. Saville claims this 'crucial fact of British history' is rarely commented on in contemporary historical writing. Saville's position is echoed in the work of another Marxist: 'It is not incorrect to regard the way in which these conditions were prepared in Britain, especially in England, as being the classic case. It was also a unique one; nowhere else were the conditions precisely reproduced; nowhere else did agrarian relations, by the eighteenth century, conform so exactly with the requirements of industrial capitalism ... In England the transformation of feudalism began early and conditions rapidly became favourable for the strengthening of the forces of the market and individual possessiveness. Partly owing to the changes which the feudal class underwent through its internecine conflicts and its ability to strengthen its power in relation to the Crown, it adapted itself to the commercial possibilities which opened up in the sixteenth century. The disintegration of the peasant community began early and its position steadily weakened while the lords were extending their control over their estates and viewing them increasingly as a commercial proposition.' T. Kemp, *Industrialisation in Nineteenth-century Europe*, Longman, 1985, p. 38.

32 Fetishism arises from the fact that natural objects assume properties which have nothing whatsoever to do with their nature but are entirely the product of the social relations of which these are a part and an expression. That such 'things' do acquire such power is no mere illusion, no simple product of the inadequate thinking of individuals, and therefore something to be 'demystified' by the power of thought alone. For Marx, fetishism arose from the very nature of capitalist

production itself – wherein the social relations between individuals and classes take the form of, become attached to, inanimate objects. Thus is wasn't the machine that brought about a social transformation in the eighteenth and early nineteenth century but the fact that such machines took the form of *capital*, that is they were privately owned and confronted a class of wage labourers.

33 For example: Daniel Bell, *The End of Ideology*, Collier-Macmillan, 1965; J. K. Galbraith, *The New Industrial State*, Hamish Hamilton, 1967; and Raymond Aron, *The Industrial System*, Weidenfeld and Nicolson, 1967.

34 For a stinging riposte to such theories and their later development, see Istvan Meszaros, *The Power of Ideology*, Harvester Wheatsheaf, 1989, especially pp. 60–177.

35 Ernest Mandel, *Marxist Economic Theory*, Merlin, 1968, p. 605. Contrary to what Mandel says, the history of capitalism has been characterised by *continual* changes that have brought first one and then another industrial sector to the fore. Thus its was textiles, cotton in particular, that occupied the pioneering role; at a later stage heavy industry – concentrated on iron and steel; and it was subsequent developments in the engineering and chemical industries that later made new means of transportation possible, especially the motor car. Mandel is guilty of more than a smack of 'technological determinism' that was characteristic of 'Marxism' in its Stalinist perversion. Kenneth Smith is certainly nearer the truth when he writes: 'The so-called "industrial revolution" actually had precious little that was industrial about it in a technological sense: it consisted to a great extent of changes in the organisation and management of work, in new methods of marketing, finance and the control of enterprises.' Kenneth Smith, *The British Economic Crisis*, Penguin, 1984.

36 Ernest Mandel, 'Workers Under Neo-Capitalism', in Ernest Mandel and George Novak, *The Revolutionary Potential of the Working Class*, Pathfinder, 1974. Despite his doubts, this did not prevent Mandel from entitling one of his subsequent books *Late Capitalism*!

37 Marcus, *Engels, Manchester and the Working Class*, p. 226. Cf. Engels on the Chartist movement: '[The workers] demand of every one who presents himself as interested in their welfare, that he should declare himself in favour of the People's Charter as proof of the sincerity of his professions, and in so doing, they protest against all outside help, for the Charter is a demand for the power to help themselves' (4: 566–7).

38 'Britain gave the world Chartism, the first broad, truly mass and political organised proletarian revolutionary movement' (*LCW* 29, p. 309).

39 These conceptions find more than an echo in Lenin's later statement about the relationship of the Bolshevik party in pre-1917 Russia with the mass movement. In *Left Wing Communism*, Lenin explained that one of the keys to the success of the Bolsheviks was its ability to merge, 'in a certain measure', with the mass movement.

40 Cited in *LCW* 5.
41 E. J. Hobsbawm, 'Introduction' to Engels, *The Condition of the Working Class*, Panther, 1969, p. 17.

4. Poverty, Crime and Politics: Engels and the Crime Question

John Lea

THE PRESENT PERIOD is an appropriate one in which to reread Engels's *The Condition of the Working Class in England*. The demolition of the welfare state under conditions of high global unemployment and dramatic increases in poverty would have been thought impossible 20 years ago. Capitalism appears, in this and other respects, to be moving backwards, closer to the world described by Engels in 1844 rather than away from it. Of course there is a wealth of literature and social science research studying and documenting these conditions and proposing various solutions. But in most of this literature the poor, the unemployed, remain passive victims of circumstance or even responsible for their own fate. To the extent that they are seen to act, it is usually in the guise of the threatening 'underclass' through the negativity of crime and violence. But this is not how Engels saw the suffering masses in 1844. As Lenin remarked:

> Even before Engels, many people had described the sufferings of the proletariat and had pointed to the necessity of helping it. Engels was the *first* to say that the proletariat is not only a suffering class; that it is in fact, the disgraceful economic condition of the proletariat that drives it irresistibly forward and compels it to fight for its ultimate emancipation. And the fighting proletariat *will help itself*. (LCW 4: 22)

It is here that one of the most important reasons for rereading Engels's book is to be found. What appears refreshingly new and relevant for us today about Engels is his method, his understanding of the suffering masses as not just objects to be studied and helped but, in the last analysis, as acting subjects, the bearers of the solution to their own problems through a historical transformation that only they can achieve. Even if his predictions of revolutionary trans-

84

formation were premature and, even if we understand that today there are new and different obstacles to their realisation, Engels's perspective appears increasingly less dated as time passes. This is underlined by a second feature of the present crisis: the combination of rising poverty and misery, with a collapse not just of traditional welfare state policies but, at a much more fundamental level, of popular confidence in the ability of politicians and political parties, of the left as well as the right, to actually do anything about it. The supposed passivity of the poor is a distorted reflection of the impotence of the politicians.

Many of these issues are brought into focus by the discussion of working-class crime in the pages of *The Condition*. The high incidence of crime among the most exploited sections of the working class seems to encapsulate all the problems facing any view of the poor as the agents of their own emancipation. Theft or assault may well be a response to oppression and exploitation but it is only occasionally directed at the actual source of such oppression. More often the victim is, like the offender, poor and powerless. Marxists for this reason have often regarded crime as a marginal issue seeing it, for example, as a feature of the 'lumpenproletariat' rather than the working class,[1] deconstructing discourses about crime as adoption of the ideological categories of bourgeois law,[2] or regarding talk of working-class crime as capitulation to 'moral panic' fuelled by the mass media.[3] A great deal of confusion is indeed created by talking generally about 'crime', a legal term which can cover everything from financial fraud to serial murder, and without paying precise attention to the social and political forces which determine which activities become criminalised in particular historical periods. When these are taken into account crime can return as a central element in the history of working-class self-activity. As the work of Marxist historians, such as Edward Thompson, Douglas Hay, Peter Linebaugh and others,[4] has shown, crime and punishment were central issues in the formation of the working class during the eighteenth century. But what was at issue was not 'crime' in some general abstract sense, but the criminalisation, by the ruling classes and the judiciary, of working-class resistance to the development of capitalist property relations.

Engels was writing, at first hand, of the experience of the working class in the next period in the development of British capitalism, the new urban factory system as represented in particular by Manchester. His discussion of crime is more attuned to the issues of urban deprivation and poverty familiar – and increasingly so – to us today. If the eighteenth century, as studied by Thompson and his collaborators, was characterised by crime *as a form* of politics, the early nineteenth century, as documented by Engels, was characterised by the transition from crime *to* politics as the form of working-class self-activity in response to capitalism.[5] In the remainder of this chapter I shall first attempt a summary of Engels' treatment of crime in *The Condition* and then discuss its relevance for today.

The nature and causes of crime

SOME YEARS AGO Jock Young summarised Engels's views on crime as amounting to four alternatives facing the impoverished worker. He '... can become so brutalised as to be, in effect, a determined creature'. Secondly, he can 'accept the prevalent mores of capitalist society, and enter into the war of all against all'. Thirdly, he can steal the property of the rich. Finally he can struggle for socialism.[6] This classification provides a very useful starting point for an investigation of Engels's treatment of crime.

Crime and brutalisation

The theme of demoralisation and brutalisation of the working class as a cause of crime is undoubtedly strong in Engels. At first sight the relation between brutalisation and crime appears to take a strongly determinist form.

> If the influences demoralising to the working-man act more powerfully, more concentratedly than usual, he becomes an offender as certainly as water abandons the fluid for the vaporous state at 80 degrees, Réamur. Under the brutal and brutalising treatment of the bourgeoisie, the working-man becomes precisely as much a thing without volition as water, and is subject to the laws of Nature with precisely the same necessity; at a certain point all freedom ceases. Hence with the extension of the proletariat, crime has increased in England and the British nation has become the most criminal in Europe. (4: 425)

Engels elaborates the effects of brutalisation in a number of directions. Moral disintegration appears to be one consequence. Lack of moral restraint combined with poverty lead inexorably to crime.

> The moral training which is not given to the worker in school is not supplied by the other conditions of his life ... his whole position and environment involves the strongest temptation to immorality. He is poor, life offers him no charm, almost every enjoyment is denied him, the penalities of the law have no further terrors for him: why should he restrain his desires, why leave to

the rich the enjoyment of his birthright, why not seize a part of it for himself? What inducement has the proletarian not to steal? ... And, when the poverty of the proletarian is intensified to the point of actual lack of the barest necessaries of life, to want and hunger, the temptation to disregard all social order does but gain power ... Want leaves the working-man the choice between starving slowly, killing himself speedily, or taking what he needs where he finds it – in plain English, stealing. (4: 412)

Engels gives us some graphic portrayals of the moral disintegration of working class life in early capitalism. Such brutal conditions are particularly concentrated in the most marginalised elements, those on the fringes of the reserve army of labour who lead a casual existence and are forced into the lodging houses and hostels. Of the London lodging houses, he wrote:

Into every bed four, five, or six human beings are piled, as many as can be packed in, sick and well, young and old, drunk and sober, men and women, just as they come, indiscriminately. Then come strife, blows, wounds, or, if these bedfellows agree, so much the worse; thefts are arranged and things done which our language, grown more humane than our deeds, refuses to accord. (4: 336)

And again, in the Manchester lodging houses:

What physical and moral atmosphere reigns in these holes I need not state. Each of these houses is a focus of crime, the scene of deeds against which human nature revolts, which would perhaps never have been executed but for this forced centralisation of vice. (4: 366)

But brutalisation and demoralisation not only affect the poorest elements in the lodging houses – they affect the working class as a whole. In this context it is important to note that although property crime has a special significance, which we shall come to, Engels does not ignore other forms of crime. In particular he pays attention to prostitution, sexual harassment and domestic violence as features of working-class family and working life. 'Next to intemperance in the enjoyment of intoxicating liquors, one of the principal faults of English working-men is sexual licence' (4: 423). The working class, 'with no means of making fitting use of its freedom' turns to drink and sex which are carried to excess (4: 423). This excess is related to poverty and insecurity: what is the point in deferred gratification and 'respectability' when there is no security in life (4: 424)?

All this sounds very similar to those middle-class Victorian moralists who studied the poor and the 'dangerous class' from the standpoint of the need to inculcate moral restraint. Thus Henry Mayhew, 20 years after Engels, in his *London Labour and the London Poor*, published in 1861, was concerned with the 'undeserving poor' as 'a vast heap of social refuse' possessed of an 'innate love of a life of ease' and criminals as 'those who will not work'. The obsession of the early Victorian middle classes in the 1830s and 1840s had been with the 'lack of moral restraint' of the working classes, and the need to habituate them to the discipline and sobriety of hard work even if this meant reforming the worst excesses of the factory system. Engels was concerned to show that the destruction of morality was precisely a product of the 'hard work' and accompanying destruction of family life imposed by capitalism itself:

> The husband works the whole day through, perhaps the wife and also the elder children, all in different places; they meet night and morning only, all under perpetual temptation to drink; what family life is possible under such conditions? Yet the working-man cannot escape from the family, must live in the family, and the consequence is a perpetual succession of family troubles, domestic quarrels, most demoralising for parents and children alike. Neglect of all domestic duties, neglect of the children, especially, is only too common among the English working people ... (4: 424–5)

Part of these strains and stresses of working-class family life are related to the condition of various family members in the labour market:

> In many cases the family is not wholly dissolved by the employment of the wife, but turned upside down. The wife supports the family, the husband sits at home, tends the children, sweeps the room and cooks. This case happens very frequently; in Manchester alone, many hundred such men could be cited, condemned to domestic occupations. It is easy to imagine the wrath aroused among the working-men by this reversal of all relations within the family, while other social conditions remain unchanged. (4: 438)

He traces similar consequences from the employment of children. Engels at first sight seems to be sanctioning a particular family division of labour and seeing domestic labour as trivial. Indeed in the German editions of 1845 and 1892 the phrase 'the wrath aroused ... relations within the family' is put in stronger language as 'the just wrath aroused among the working-men by this virtual castration, and the reversal of all relations within the family'. There were plenty of middle-class reformers lamenting the effects of the factory system on the morality and family life of the working classes. But the comment 'while other social conditions remain un-changed' implies that Engels starts from the possibility of a 'demo-cratic domesticity' advocated by feminists[7] where the capitalist ideol-ogy of the male as breadwinner has been overcome:

> And yet this condition, which unsexes the man and takes from the woman all womanliness without being able to bestow upon the man true womanliness, or the woman true manliness – this condition which degrades, in the most shameful way, both sexes, and, through them, Humanity ... we must admit that so total a reversal of the position of the sexes can have come to pass only because the sexes have been placed in a false position from the beginning. If the reign of the wife over the husband, as inevitably brought about by the factory system, is inhuman, the pristine rule of the husband over the wife must have been inhuman too. If the wife can now base her supremacy upon the fact that she supplies the greater part, nay, the whole of the common possession, the necessary inference is that this community of possession is no true and rational one, since one member of the family boasts offensively of contributing the greater share. If the family of our present society is being thus dissolved, this dissolution merely shows that, at bottom, the binding tie of this family was not family affection, but private interest lurking under cloak of a pre-tended community of possessions. (4: 439)

The first moment or aspect, then, of Engels's treatment of working-class crime is the purely negative one of brutalisation and the deterio-ration of family life. Obviously, if this theme of brutalisation is ab-stracted out from the rest of Engels's work as a 'theory of the causes of crime' then we end up with something very similar to conventional sociology or criminology. In the same way, his account could be seen to echo the sentiments of middle-class reformers of the factory system. But this was not Engels's intention.

The war of all against all

A second theme in the discussion of the causes of crime focuses on the social relations of competitive capitalist accumulation which have brought England to a state of the war of all against all.

> The brutal indifference, the unfeeling isolation of each in his pri-vate interest ... The dissolution of mankind into monads, of which each one has a separate principle, the world of atoms, is here carried out to its utmost extreme.
> Hence it comes, too, that the social war, the war of each

against all, is here openly declared. Just as in Stirner's recent book,[8] people regard each other only as useful objects; each exploits the other and the end of it all is that the stronger treads the weaker under foot ... (4: 329)

At times Engels's discussion almost has the flavour of a conservative romanticism lamenting the decline of a stable, ordered society in which each individual knew his or her place:

The very turmoil of the streets has something repulsive, something against which human nature rebels. The hundreds of thousands of all classes and ranks crowding past each other, are they not human beings with the same qualities and powers, and with the same interest in being happy? ... And still they crowd by one another as though they had nothing in common, nothing to do with one another ... The dissolution of mankind into monads, of which each one has a separate principle, the world of atoms, is here carried out to its utmost extreme. (4: 329)

Bourgeois critics of the new urban life were of course saying similar things. Thus in the same year of publication of Engels's book, 1844, the Tory *Blackwoods Magazine* warned that 'the restraints of character, relationship and vicinity are ... lost in the crowd ... Multitudes remove responsibility without weakening passion.'[9] But unlike these critics of the *anomie* of the industrial city, Engels is clear that is it capital accumulation that lies behind this process, and which inevitably imposes its effects upon the working class:

Since capital, the direct or indirect control of the means of subsistence and production, is the weapon with which this social warfare is carried on, it is clear that all the disadvantages of such a state must fall upon the poor ... If the worker can get no work he may steal, if he is not afraid of the police, or starve, in which case the police will take care that he does so in a quiet and inoffensive manner. (4: 330)

Crime is the natural result:

In this country, social war is under full headway, every one stands for himself, and fights for himself against all comers, and whether or not he shall injure all the others who are his declared foes, depends upon a cynical calculation as to what is most advantageous for himself. It no longer occurs to any one to come to a peaceful understanding with his fellow-man; all differences are settled by threats, violence, or in a law court ... And this war grows from year to year, as the criminal tables show, more violent, passionate, irreconcilable ... This war of each against all, of the bourgeoisie against the proletariat, need cause us no surprise, for it is only the logical sequel of the principle involved in free competition. (4: 427)

Crime as the inevitable result of capitalist social relations had been stressed by Engels in his *Outlines of a Critique of Political Economy* published the year before:

Competition governs the numerical advance of mankind; it likewise governs its moral advance. Anyone who has any knowledge of the statistics of crime must have been struck by the peculiar regularity with which crime advances year by year, and with which certain causes produce certain crimes. The extension of the factory system is followed everywhere by an increase in crime ... This regularity proves that crime, too, is governed by competition; that society creates a *demand* for crime which is met by a corresponding *supply*; that the gap created by the arrest, transportation or execution of a certain number is at once filled by others, just as every gap in population is at once filled by new arrivals; in other words, that crime presses on the means of punishment just as the people press on the means of employment. How just it is to punish criminals under these circumstances, quite apart from any other considerations, I leave to the judgement of my readers. (3: 442)

In seeing crime as the natural result of capitalist relations of production Engels was far ahead of both those modern criminologists who insist on seeing crime as the result of some type of disruption of normal social relations and those who see it simply as a result of some 'moral panic' induced by the mass media. For Engels, crime is not a result of the breakdown of social relations, it is rather one of the necessary forms they take. As Steven Marcus, in his biography of Engels in Manchester, wrote, crime is not considered by Engels to be a result of deviance or the absence of norms:

It is, in the first place, much too intimately connected with the values and norms it violates to be considered as simply anomic in respect to them; and secondly, no behaviour that is both an inversion and a parody of another can be properly or fully understood as a deviant form of the latter.[10]

That crime arises from the normal workings of capitalist production rather than their breakdown is even clearer when Engels comes to talk about the criminal activities of the bourgeoisie itself, an area with which many modern criminologists have had problems precisely because it is frequently impossible to find anything 'deviant' about the bourgeois criminal.[11] Much of this activity, especially on the part of the small bourgeoisie, merchants and shopkeepers, concerned the adulteration of foodstuffs. Thus 'The workers get what is too bad for the property-holding class ...' (4: 368), that is, low-quality rotting vegetables, meat, etc. Engels quotes cases of the Manchester courts fining meat-sellers for sale of tainted meat (4: 369). He concludes:

> And when one reflects upon the many cases which must escape detection in the extensive markets that stretch along the front of every main street, under the slender supervision of the market inspectors – and how else can one explain the boldness with which whole animals are exposed for sale? – when one considers how great the temptation must be, in view of the incomprehensibly small fines mentioned in the foregoing cases; when one reflects what condition a piece of meat must have reached to be seized by the inspectors, it is impossible to believe that the workers obtain good and nourishing meat as a usual thing. (4: 369–70)

But workers are 'victimised in yet another way by the money-greed of the middle class' (4: 370). Engels quotes the local *Liverpool Mercury* on cases describing all the fiddles of the period – sugar adulterated with pounded rice, refuse from soap being sold as sugar, cocoa adulterated with brown earth and mutton fat, recycled tea leaves, flour adulterated with gypsum and chalk, and so on. Not only food was involved but cloth, pottery and various quack medicines, such as the notorious Godfrey's Cordial.

> Fraud is practised in the sale of articles of every sort ... But the lion's share of the evil results of these frauds falls to the workers. The rich are less deceived, because they can pay the high prices of the large shops which have a reputation to lose ... while ... They [the workers] must deal with the small retailers, must perhaps buy on credit, and these small retail dealers who cannot sell even the same quality of goods so cheaply as the largest retailers, because of their small capital and the large proportional expenses of their business, must knowingly or unknowingly buy adulterated goods in order to sell at the lower prices required, and to meet the competition of the others. (4: 371)

Engels thus had a sophisticated understanding of the contemporary dynamics of fraud committed against the working class as consumer – small retailers had little choice but to adulterate, since these were the competitive conditions. If discovered they could always move elsewhere, whereas a large shop would lose its capital if it was exposed.

The crime of the petty bourgeois in food adulteration, etc. is understood as an inevitable consequence of the market.

The crimes of the bourgeoisie did not stop at fraud and adulteration of course. Engels was mainly concerned with the conditions of the working class, he was not writing a treatise on criminology. For a history of murder among the upper classes we turn elsewhere. Engels's focus was on those crimes committed against the poor and the working class, and in this context he mentions another form of crime, sexual harassment and rape at work, in a context in which modern writers would describe as 'power rape' or 'exploitation rape'.[12]

> It is, besides, a matter of course that factory servitude, like any other, and to an even higher degree, confers the *jus primae noctis* upon the master. In this respect also the employer is sovereign over the persons and charms of his employees. The threat of discharge suffices to overcome all resistance in nine cases out of ten, if not in ninety-nine out of a hundred, in girls who, in any case, have no strong indictments to chastity. If the master is mean enough ... his mill is also his harem; and the fact that not all manufacturers use their power, does not in the least change the position of the girls. In the beginning of manufacturing industry, when most of the employers were upstarts without education or consideration for the hypocrisy of society, they let nothing interfere with the exercise of their vested rights. (4: 441–2)

Engels's discussion finally moves on to wider crimes of the bourgeoisie which includes death in the city by asphyxiation and workplace death in the factories and mills, by what would now politely and equally hypocritically be called 'industrial accidents', in many cases brought about by the use of drugs to pacify children at work (4: 436–7)

Up to this point Engels has given us a graphic portrayal of crime as pure negativity, of the working class as suffering from the moral and social disintegration inflicted by industrial capitalism of which interpersonal violence and theft, inflicted by working-class people on one another, is the natural result. He has also shown how the capitalist class, in the normal course of business, is under constant pressure to violate laws and to engage in criminal, as well as legal, exploitation of working-class communities. If his account had stopped here, he would still have given us a graphic historical memoire of the conditions of life in early industrial capitalism. If he had been among the liberal utilitarian reformers of his age, such as Edwin Chadwick or Henry Mayhew, he would then have gone on to suggest various enlightened strategies for the moral education of the working classes and the amelioration of their conditions. But Engels's interests lay in quite other directions.

Crime and the struggle for socialism

For Engels, as for Marx, any amelioration of the conditions of the working class brought about from above, by the actions of the ruling class and the state, would be concessions wrung on the basis of fear of the self-activity of the class and its latent, and growing, capacity to overthrow capitalism. Engels was not, therefore, concerned with Victorian plans for social reform but with understanding how, from the conditions of demoralisation and deprivation described so far, the working class emerges as a historical force. For Engels, crime is a central part of this emergence. It is not just that the working class leaves crime behind as it develops political consciousness, crime is an essential stage in the development of class consciousness. Class consciousness and working-class political organisation overcome the limitations of (certain forms of) crime while preserving some of their driving forces, notably the sense of rage and hatred of capitalism. Politics is the dialectical transcendence of crime, not simply its displacement.

The demoralisation and brutalisation of the workers finds its immediate negation in rage and hatred:

> There is, therefore, no cause for surprise if the workers, treated as brutes, actually become such; or if they can maintain their consciousness of manhood only by cherishing the most glowing hatred, the most unbroken inward rebellion against the bourgeoisie in power. (4: 411)

Such hatred, although expressed through crime, was for Engels '... the proof that the workers feel the inhumanity of their position, that they refuse to be degraded to the level of brutes, and that they will one day free themselves from servitude to the bourgeoisie' (4: 414). The consequence is crime which is, of course, a destructive activity. The working class has been negated, and crime is where it discovers its power and humanity but at first only in that negation, by negating others even within its own ranks. In other words '... such crime is estranged labour coming to perverse life, endeavouring immediately to cancel its frozen and "objectified" existence and behave in accordance with its deformed conception of a free human being'.[13] But as the workers come to realise the source of their oppression, the more conscious among them come to direct their rage against its real source rather than against their fellow workers. This involves initially a focus on theft which according to Engels is becoming the majority form of crime committed by the poor: 'The offences, as in all civilised countries, are, in the great majority of cases against property and have, therefore, arisen from want in some form; for what a man has, he does not steal.' (4: 426). That the development of capitalism brings a relative shift from violence to theft in inter-personal crime would find agreement among many historians[14] though it is obvious that various forms of violence – against women in the home for example – would be under-represented in the arrest or reported crime statistics and theft against property owners well represented.

But as capitalism develops the working class becomes aware of itself as a class, rather than as a group of individuals. The workers overcome the individual demoralisation and brutalisation which finds its reflection in individual crime against property. The rage against and hatred of the bourgeoisie, which took an individual form in crimes against property, takes on a more directed, organised, effec-tive political form as the working class makes the transition from being simply a class-in-itself to a class-for-itself. Engels describes the process in the following way:

> The earliest, crudest, and least fruitful form of this rebellion was that of crime. The working-man lived in poverty and want, and saw that others were better off than he. It was not clear to his mind why he, who did more for society than the rich idler, should be the one to suffer under these conditions. Want con-quered his inherited respect for the sacredness of property, and he stole ...
>
> The workers soon realised that crime did not help matters. The criminal could protest against the existing order of society only singly, as one individual; the whole might of society was brought to bear upon each criminal, and crushed him with its immense superiority. Besides, theft was the most primitive form of protest, and for this reason, if for no other, it never became the universal expression of the public opinion of the working-men, however much they might approve of it in silence. (4: 502–3)

How does such a transition, from crime to politics, from Luddite machine-smashing and robbery to Chartism and Socialism, become possible? Obviously through capitalist development, the expansion of industry and the size of the working class, the decasualisation of the labour market, the reduction in female and child labour and the stabilisation of the working-class family and community: all these factors lay at the basis of the emergence of strong working-class political and trade union organisation for the collective organisation of grievances on one hand and the development of strong informal controls against crime within the community on the other. But this is to move ahead, well beyond the period about which Engels was writing, and to read into his account a social history of the growth of a type of working-class community and Labour politics which he did not, at that time, anticipate. In particular such a view would see criminality as a sort of pre-history rather than an essential moment in the development of class consciousness. In fact both Engels and his collaborator Marx were thinking, in the mid-1840s, of something very different: the proximity of revolution. The growing power of the Chartist movement coupled with violent resistance by the employers to trades unionism convinced both Engels and Marx that a revolutionary situation was near at hand.

> When such insanity prevails in the property-holding class, when it is so blinded by its momentary profit that it no longer has eyes for the most conspicuous signs of the times, surely all hope of a peaceful solution of the social question for England must be abandoned. The only possible solution is a violent revolution, which cannot fail to take place. (4: 547)

And furthermore:

> The classes are divided more and more sharply, the spirit of resistance penetrates the workers, the bitterness intensifies, the guerrilla skirmishes become concentrated in more important battles, and soon a slight impulse will suffice to set the avalanche in motion. Then, indeed, will the war-cry resound through the land: 'War to the mansion, peace to the cottage' – but then it will be too late for the rich to beware. (4: 583)

Engels quotes the criminal arrest statistics for England and Wales which rise consistently from 4,605 in 1805, through 14,437 in 1825, to 31,309 in 1842. In Scotland an even more rapid increase was to be noted. Engels emphasises the urban nature of the bulk of these arrests – London and Manchester produced a quarter of the whole in 1842. He also notes that nearly all crime arises within the proletariat, over half of those arrested could read or write only imperfectly, and a third could neither read nor write. Out of 100, 0.22 had a higher education. He continues:

> If demoralisation and crime multiply twenty years longer in this proportion (and if English manufacture in these twenty years should be less prosperous than heretofore, the progressive multiplication of crime can only continue the more rapidly), what will the result be? Society is already in a state of visible dissolution ... (4: 426)

Thus as the social war between bourgeoisie and proletariat continues to intensify, it would continue to take the form of both rising criminality and at the same time the metamorphosis of criminality into more organised forms of class struggle. As long as it is under-

stood that crime and organised class struggle, far from being mutually exclusive, are components of each other's development – crime
as a primitive form of class war, heightened class struggle as
increasing the rage that gives rise to crime – then we can understand why Engels saw it as natural to presuppose that both would
increase, hand in hand. To make sense of this assumption two
things have to be understood.

Firstly, it is important not to make the mistake of reading Engels'
account, written in the 1840s, from the standpoint of modern notions
of criminality which already presuppose the modern criminal law and a
clear distinction between organised reformist working-class politics
and crime.[15] The criminality which Engels has in mind is much closer
to what Edward Thompson and his collaborators called 'social
crime',[16] much of which arose from the defence of older forms of
traditional rights – to common pasture for example – against the
encroachment of bourgeois property relations and which continued
into the urban setting in such forms as traditions of 'pilferage' in the
London Docks. This is the crime that working-class people 'approve of
in silence' and not the modern notion of petty crime, stealing from
your neighbours or robbing elderly people, crimes of which the working class, then and now, firmly disapproves. Most important of all it
has to be remembered that attempts at the formation of trade unions,
then termed 'combinations', was itself a criminal activity, under the
notorious Combination Acts of 1799 and 1800. The criminalisation of
working-class resistance to capitalist property relations in the eighteenth century was followed by the criminalisation of working-class
resistance within capitalist property relations in the early nineteenth
century. But it is important also to understand that a clear distinction
between social crime and harmful intra-class crime is one imposed by
historians after the event. The distinction at the time was much more
blurred. As E. P. Thompson warned: 'there is not "nice" social crime
here and "nasty" anti-social crime there'.[17] Such a distinction presupposes the strong cohesive working-class community which was as yet
in a process of formation.[18] This is precisely what is implied in crime
as a moment in the development of class consciousness.

A second factor to keep in mind is that Engels is not engaging in
some sort of romanticisation of a criminal underworld or 'lumpenproletariat' as the leading force in the class struggle, nor is he
regarding personal crimes like rape, for example, as somehow class-
conscious acts. Engels is clearly talking about crimes committed by
the working class against the bourgeoisie, a type of criminality
which, as already noted, mainly concerned theft, though arson and
machine-smashing are also mentioned. While Marx and Engels did
not always use the term 'lumpenproletariat' precisely in a sociologi-
cal sense,[19] it was clearly distinguished from the working class,
including the most marginalised sections of the reserve army of the

unemployed. Four years later, in the *Communist Manifesto* (1848), Marx and Engels referred to the

> ... 'dangerous class', the social scum, the passively rotting mass thrown off by the lowest layers of the old society ... [which] ... may, here and there swept into the movement by a proletarian revolution, its conditions of life, however, prepare it far more for the part of a bribed tool of reactionary regimes.[20]

Of course, the brutalisation by capitalism, to which theft is a response, also gives rise to more destructive forms of inter-personal violence within the working class, and it is in this context that some of Engels's more chauvinist remarks concerning Irish immigrant workers have to be read. It is also of course true that in the early nineteenth century, as the working class was still in the process of formation, the distinction between the living conditions of its poorest sections, so graphically documented in *The Condition*, and those of the lumpenproletariat or criminal underworld is blurred.

> This reserve army, which embraces an immense multitude during the crisis and a large number during the period which may be regarded as the average between the highest prosperity and the crisis, is the 'surplus population' of England, which keeps body and soul together by begging, stealing, street-sweeping, collecting manure, pushing hard-carts, driving donkeys, peddling, or performing occasional small jobs. (4: 384)

This is echoed later by Marx in *Capital* where the poorest sections of the reserve army of labour are seen as living in similar conditions to, though distinct from, the criminal underworld:

> The lowest sediment of the relative surplus population, finally, dwells in the sphere of pauperism. Exclusive of vagabonds, criminals, prostitutes, in a word, the 'dangerous classes'[21] this layer of society consists of ... First, those able to work ... Second, orphans and pauper children ... Third, the demoralised and ragged and those unable to work ... [22]

The fact that the actual conditions of life of sections of the reserve army of labour blur into the lumpenproletariat is the other side of the coin of the criminalisation, by the ruling class, of the working class in general in the late eighteenth and early nineteenth centuries as 'the mob'.[23] But however similar the conditions of life of sections of the working class and the criminal underworld, the political distinction between these groups remains profound. The distinguishing feature of the working class – even the weaker sections of it continually moving in and out of the ranks of the reserve army of labour – is its capacity to learn and develop forms of class consciousness. It is quite otherwise with that permanent underworld of professional thieves and robbers for whom crime is itself a form of economy and employment whose social relations are antipathetic to all forms of class consciousness.

These factors: crime as a form of generalised, albeit individual, resistance to capital, the working-class rather than 'lumpen' nature of much crime, together with the assumed immediate prospect of revolutionary upheaval, help explain why Engels made the assumption that crime would continue rising even as it was merging into more developed collective forms of political struggle. But history developed in a different direction.

The incidence of crime

THE QUESTION OF crime rates during the latter half of the last century seems to have been something of a problem both for socialists and conservatives. *The Condition of the Working Class in England* was, in fact, published at a turning point in the development of crime. Up to the mid-century it is reasonably clear that crime rates were rising. Most historians are agreed on this.[24] However, from around the mid-1840s crime rates fell steadily until well after the First World War.[25] According to commentators such as Lynn McDonald,[26] there was a conspiracy of silence about falling crime in the second half of the nineteenth century which embraced both the Left and Right. The Right saw rising crime both as a vindication of the breeding habits of the criminal classes and of the necessity for 'continued use of capital punishment (and fighting the abolition movement), flogging, transportation and severe prisons for children' (ibid.). For the Left, it was argued that rising crime was an essential indicator of the worsening and oppressive nature of capitalism.

According to McDonald, this position assumed the status of political dogma in the revolutionary socialist movement:

> ... a significance was given to rising crime that would make it difficult for a dedicated Marxist to question. Decreases in crime would be expected ... if the theory of the liberal bourgeoisie were right, if the post-revolutionary republic had resulted in an adequate society. But instead of 'order, harmony and love of humanity' there was 'disorder, dissension, murder, theft, bankruptcy and child abuse' ... To argue that crime was decreasing was to question the very need for communist revolution.[27]

McDonald considers that 'Engels himself provided the kernel of a

revised position' by showing that crime was a stage in the development of class consciousness and that the workers gradually made
the shift to organised class politics. The argument here is that
Engels, if he had thought through his argument consistently, would
have realised that the development of organised class politics would
have led to a decrease in crime. As I have argued above, this is a
mistaken view of Engels's original argument concerning the dynamic
relation between criminality and revolutionary struggle as he saw
them in the 1840s. What he failed to anticipate was not the growth
of working-class political organisation but the particular processes of
the 'stabilisation' of capitalist society which introduced a relationship between crime and politics quite different to that which he had
originally envisaged. There were several elements involved.

Firstly, the development of the tradition of reformist trade unionism led by the skilled workers drives a wedge between crime and
politics in the sense understood by Engels. Social crime never of
course entirely disappears from working-class communities, and a
healthy tradition of things 'falling off the back of a lorry' continues to
the present time. But gradually theft and violence come to assume
their modern forms of largely intra-class crime in which individual
criminal acts against bourgeois property or its defenders, except at
times of major strikes or lockouts, becomes more concentrated among
marginalised members of the reserve army of the unemployed.

A second important factor is the increasing segregation between
the classes in modern cities. Engels in fact observes the beginning of
this process and spends some time considering its implications in
the context of the anticipated climax of the class struggle. Thus he
wonders aloud why the bourgeoisie is so calm in the face of the
rising crime wave and accuses them of 'mad blindness' arising from
its 'class prejudice and preconceived opinions' (4: 427).

> But it may well surprise us that the bourgeoisie remains so quiet
> and composed in the face of the rapidly gathering storm clouds, that
> it can read all these things daily in the papers without, we will not
> say indignation at such a social condition, but fear of its conse-
> quences, of a universal outburst of that which manifests itself symp-
> tomatically from day to day in the form of crime. (4: 427)

Engels partly answers his question by grasping the role of the city in
enclosing and segregating social problems. As long as they remain
within their own suburbs, the rich are shielded from crime, while
the poor have only other poor people for their victims. The Manchester slums hide their poverty:

> True, poverty often dwells in hidden alleys close to the palaces of
> the rich; but, in general, a separate territory has been assigned to

it, where, removed from the sight of the happier classes, it may struggle along as it can. (4: 331)

The town itself is peculiarly built, so that a person may live in it for years, and go in and out daily without coming into contact with a working-people's quarter or even with workers, that is, so long as he confines himself to his business or to pleasure walks. (4: 347–8)

He describes the division of Manchester into the central business district with main roads and busy traffic but no residents and where at night 'only watchmen and policemen traverse its narrow lanes with their dark lanterns', surrounded by the working class districts and then, as an outer 'girdle' the upper and middle bourgeoisie:

And the finest part of the arrangement is this, that members of this money aristocracy can take the shortest road through the middle of all the labouring districts to their places of business without ever seeing that they are in the midst of the grimy misery that lurks to the right and the left. For the thoroughfares leading from the [Manchester] Exchange in all directions out of the city are lined, on both sides, with an almost unbroken series of shops, and are so kept in the hands of the middle and lower bourgeoisie, which, out of self interest, cares for a decent and cleanly external existence and *can* care for it. (4: 348)

This middle-class flight to the suburbs accentuated after 1870 and, notwithstanding a growing middle-class fear of urban public order (in London particularly) at the time of the unemployed riots of 1885[28] and the Jack the Ripper murders of the later 1880s, such social shifts had the effect of reducing working-class crime against the bourgeoisie and increasing the relative proportion of such crime which was inflicted within the working-class community itself. At the same time, however, the strengthening of working-class neighbourhood and community organisation, evident towards the end of the nineteenth century,[29] contributed to the general tendency of crime to fall during the latter part of the nineteenth century.

Finally, Engels was writing at that historical moment when the criminal justice agencies of the bourgeois state were about to begin their incursion, accompanied by railway building and urban planning, into the hitherto no-go working-class areas of the city and to bring working-class petty criminality under its dominion. To a considerable extent, up until the 1850s, the working class and the poor were left to deal themselves with crime whose victims were within their own communities[30] with the consequence that, while there was plenty of 'intra-class' crime in Engels's day, as we have seen, a much greater proportion of the crime that came before the Justices of the Peace was 'inter-class' crime, more closely related to the war waged by the proletariat against the bourgeoisie. The effect of the gradual but successful penetration of the police into the working-class communities by the turn of the century[31] was to reduce the latter to the role of 'informal social control' of crime and other forms of deviance.

Thus the 'modern' system was consolidated. Crime and politics parted company, the latter becoming less a matter of individualised class warfare and more the petty and destructive behaviour which sections of the lower working class inflict upon one another, while the criminal justice system, by securing its symbolic monopoly over the public control of such crime and disposal of its perpetrators, achieved a further solidification of its hegemony. The equality of the rule of law – while not without considerable benefits to the working class – becomes a form of domination akin to that of capital itself, in which the equality between the parties to a contract is the starting point for subordination. By claiming to deal impartially with the violence and theft inflicted on all social classes, by equating the violence of the weak with that of the powerful, the criminal law completes its transition from the ideology of direct class rule of the eighteenth century, described by Douglas Hay,[32] to that of indirect class rule through the regulation of general 'criminality'.

Engels and the present crisis

THE CONDITION WAS written, not on the eve of revolution, but on the threshold of a long period of capitalist growth and relative stability which continued, despite periodic economic crises, until the First World War and the Russian Revolution. After the crisis of the inter-war years, a new period of stability followed the Second World War before giving way, in the 1970s, to the present period of increasing social and economic crisis. The thesis that capitalism, from an initially progressive role in developing the forces of production and culture, eventually becomes a fetter on human progress is a central component of historical materialism, though it is clear that both Marx and Engels underestimated the time period over which such a process would mature.[33] A discussion of the general dynamics of such decay and how they might be seen to manifest themselves in modern capitalism is beyond our discussion here. However, one important indicator of such decay might be found in long-term tendencies in crime rates.

Students of long-term trends in the incidence of homicide, robbery and other violent crime have suggested the hypothesis of a

'U-curve' in which crime rates in leading industrial capitalist
nations, England included, generally fell during the period after 1850
down to a plateau in the inter-war years, and began rising again
during the period after 1950.[34] Such a continuous rise in crime has,
of course, attracted a variety of explanations. It cannot, for example,
be explained simply as a consequence of poverty and unemployment
insofar as it was an observable tendency as much during the period
of economic expansion and relative social stability following the
Second World War as during the period of rising unemployment and
economic stagnation after the mid-1970s. However, it is clear in
retrospect that the period of the welfare state and relatively full
employment left large pockets of poverty and deprivation and at the
same time, by increasing expectations, particularly of working-class
young people, through diffusion of social rights and mass secondary
education, fostered the type of frustrations that lead to crime.[35]
Since the beginning of the 1980s the increasing inability of capitalism to sustain the welfare state, the need for an increasingly open
war by capital on all the social and political gains of the working-
class movement – which were the components of earlier stabilisation
and integration – is recreating a society of growing poverty and
inequality, long-term unemployment, particularly for young people,
and a social morality reminiscent of Engels's description of a 'social
war' in which 'everyone stands for himself'. If falling crime during
the second half of the nineteenth century was an index of capitalis-
m's ability to develop the productive forces, raise working-class
living standards and create the general foundations for social cohe-
sion, then rising crime in the second half of the twentieth century
may be an index of capitalism's exhaustion, reflected in an increasing socially and physically destructive use of technology, increasing
inequality and fragmentation of the working class and the undermining of the foundations of social stability.

It follows that any attempt to repeat Engels's analysis and see
rising crime among working-class youth today as once again the
precursor to radical consciousness must take account of the fact that
the 'same' phenomena under different social and historical circumstances may indicate quite different underlying dynamics. There are a
number of obvious differences between the period of which Engels
was writing and the present period.

On the one hand, it might seem obvious that the issue of a transition from crime to politics simply does not occur since the working
class has historically already made that transition. Any re-emergence of
radical or revolutionary consciousness in the foreseeable future will
emerge from the organised, and largely non-criminalised, sections of
the working class – and other social movements – taking advantage of
the established structures of political organisation and civil rights
based on the working-class struggles of the last century. In such a

situation the already established distinction between crime and politics will not be reversed – given the unproductiveness of crime as a form of political struggle and the fact that all the existing structures of political thought and organisation have moved beyond it. Even to pose the question is to answer it. Of course political and social movements will clash directly with the police, but only episodically and when the latter turn from their 'proper' focus on the control of crime to acting as the direct political agents of the ruling class in industrial conflicts or political demonstrations. Meanwhile the most salient aspect of crime in working-class communities is defence *against* crime: a form of mobilisation, which, while it may well draw on traditions of 'self activity', is more likely to secure a closer, if critical, relationship between the police and the working-class community.

On the other hand, the character of much crime has changed. Precisely because of the development of the organised working-class political and community structures noted above, social crime in the old sense declined. The growth of long-term unemployment and the weakening of the political strength of the working class are of course fertile conditions for the re-emergence of such activity. Indeed a redistributive illegal economy of shoplifting and stolen consumer goods never entirely disappeared in the poorest sections of the working class and has undoubtedly grown in recent years. But as a form of illegal economy it has been largely overtaken by the infinitely more profitable drugs trade.[36] Rather than being a form of social crime or collectively sanctioned popular resistance to capitalism, the global drugs economy is, on the contrary, one of the most profitable sectors of international capitalist enterprise, with its entrepreneurs, financiers, managers, and workers. It is not a matter of criminal organisations taking advantage of social crime, as eighteenth-century professional poaching gangs might have taken advantage of popular resistance to the encroachment of common land rights, but rather a matter of the hegemonisation by the 'illegal sector' of multinational capital of some of the most personally destructive and debilitating responses to the demoralisation flowing from exclusion from the labour market, and the social decay which accompanies it.

This has been accompanied by an important change in the relationship between the bottom or 'latent' section of the reserve army of labour and the lumpenproletariat: the development of virtually permanent unemployment for an increasing number of young people who have never entered the labour market and no longer function even as a 'latent' section of the reserve army of labour. They have given up even looking for work. Having few alternatives to petty crime as a source of income pushes them into the traditional criminal underworld, but at the same time as that underworld is being reorganised and subject to the discipline of (illegal) capital in the form of the drugs economy. The inner-city unemployed youth thus moves from the bottom of one labour market to the bottom of another – from the declining, increasingly casualised legal labour market to the expanding, hazardous, casualised criminal labour market, working under conditions that make the emergence of traditional forms of class consciousness difficult to imagine. Rage and anger is predominantly a reference to exclusion from, rather than resistance to, the imposition of capitalist work and consumption relations. Meanwhile working-class communities are further weakened and demoralised by the growth in debilitating interpersonal crime – theft, robbery, domestic violence and rape.

Thus making a connection between crime and political consciousness has become difficult, if not impossible. As late as the mid-1970s Stuart Hall and his colleagues could still advance a sophisticated presentation of crime as resistance. In a discussion of the involvement of unemployed black youth in street crime, they wrote:

> Crime as such is not a political act, especially where the vast number of victims are people whose class position is hardly distinguishable from that of the criminals. It is not even necessarily a 'quasi-political' act. But in certain circumstances, it *can* provide, or come to be defined as expressing some sides of an oppositional class consciousness ... it requires only a moment's reflection to see how acts of stealing, pick pocketing, snatching and robbing with violence ... can give a muffled and displaced expression to the experience of permanent exclusion.[37]

Black involvement in street crime was an issue in the 1970s and 1980s as the ethnic minority communities were the first to feel the effects of the end of post-war capitalist expansion. But by the beginning of the present decade,[38] as the issue widened out to include substantial sections of white working-class youth now surplus to capital's requirements, the mood among radicals had changed. In her discussion of young people and violent crime in various parts of Britain in the early 1990s, Beatrix Campbell[39] argued that whereas the riots in Brixton and other areas in the early 1980s had a legitimate element of grievance against police victimisation of black youth, the violence bursting out on working-class housing estates around Britain '... did not represent revolt, they were simply larger displays of what these neighbourhoods had to put up with much of the time'. And what they had been putting up with was the terrorism of organised criminal gangs of unemployed aggressive young men.

> Houses were set on fire, roofs were cleared of tiles, walls were stripped of radiators, houses were ram-raided, residents were

robbed, threatened and pestered by gangs of lads who seemed beyond society's reach. Victimisation was a way of life.[40]

Much of the discussion by the media and by social scientists has not surprisingly taken the form of a concern with the growth of the 'underclass', returning in some respects to the concerns of the early Victorian bourgeoisie with the 'lack of moral restraint' of the lower orders. From the standpoint of Engels's analysis, crime seems locked into the first, negative, stage of demoralisation and brutalisation. For the poor, and in particular long-term unemployed young people, the transition from crime to politics has been replaced by the transition from politics to crime as contact with older traditions of class organisation and struggle are lost. This time the dialectic appears to be elsewhere: crime appears as an obstacle: a problem to be solved *by* the already existing organised working-class and progressive social movements rather than a component in their own formation.

But this would be a one-sided view. The organised working-class movement, the reformist political parties and the welfare state which gave them relevance are themselves in crisis. The increasing levels of poverty, deprivation and social marginalisation which give rise to crime are part of the same forces which drive capital to demand the dismantlement of welfare rights and a recriminalisation of social protest extending from trade union action to wide categories of public gatherings.[41] It is not a question simply of the 'old' political structures getting together to mobilise and politicise those sections of the unemployed and young people turning to crime; they have showed precious little inclination to do so up till now. It is the question of new forms of organisation and new leaderships emerging within the working-class movement with the problems of crime, poverty and unemployment at the top of their agendas.

Notes

1   P. Hirst, *Law, Socialism and Democracy*, Allen Lane, 1986.
2   P. O'Malley, 'The Purpose of Knowledge: Pragmatism and the Praxis of Marxist Criminology', *Contemporary Crises*, no. 12, pp. 65–79, 1988.
3   The debate on the Left during the late 1980s concerning inner-city youth crime exhibited all these features. Some of the main texts were: S. Hall et al., *Policing the Crisis*, Macmillan, 1978; J. Lea and J. Young *What Is To Be Done about Law and Order?* 2nd edition, Pluto Press, 1993; CCCS (eds), *The Empire Strikes Back*, Hutchinson, 1982; P. Scraton (ed.) *Law, Order and the Authoritarian State*, Oxford University Press, 1987.
4   E. P. Thompson, 'The Moral Economy of the English Crowd in the Eighteenth Century', *Past and Present*, no. 50, pp. 76–136, 1967; E. P. Thompson, *Whigs and Hunters: The Origins of the Black Act*, Penguin, 1974;

D. Hay, 'Property, Authority and the Criminal Law', in D. Hay (ed.), *Albion's Fatal Tree: Crime and Society in Eighteenth Century England*, Allen Lane, 1975; Peter Linebaugh, *The London Hanged*, Allen Lane, 1991.

5 That is in no way to suggest that the period studied by Thompson and others is only of historical relevance. The criminalisation, *de facto* and *de jure*, of basic rights has featured heavily over the last few years, with the poll tax and the 1994 Criminal Justice Act, whose revisions of the law on trespass evoke Thompson's discussion of the notorious legislation of the eighteenth century.

6 J. Young, 'Working Class Criminology', in I. Taylor, P. Walton and J. Young (eds), *Critical Criminology*, Routledge and Kegan Paul, 1975, p. 78.

7 For a sympathetic appraisal of the contribution of *The Condition* from a feminist perspective, see L. Vogel, *Marxism and the Oppression of Women: Towards a Unitary Theory*, Pluto Press, 1983, especially pp. 43–8.

8 The individualist anarchist Max Stirner published his book *The Ego and His Own* in 1844.

9 'Causes of the Increase of Crime', *Blackwood's Edinburgh Magazine* 56, 1844, quoted in M. Wiener, *Reconstructing the Criminal: Culture, Law and Policy in England, 1830–1914*, Cambridge University Press, 1990, p. 19.

10 L. Marcus, *Engels and Manchester*, Weidenfeld and Nicolson, 1974, p. 223.

11 For discussions of this problem in criminology, see S. Box, *Crime, Power and Mystification*, Tavistock, 1983, Ch. 2, and Pearce, *Crimes of the Powerful*, Pluto Press, 1976.

12 Cf. Box, ibid., Ch. 4.

13 Marcus, *Engels and Manchester*, p. 221.

14 H. Zehr, *Crime and the Development of Modern Society*, Croome Helm, 1976.

15 Though, as discussed below, the distinction may be blurring again.

16 The term was coined originally by E. J. E. Hobsbawm, 'Distinctions between socio-political and other forms of crime', *Society for the Study of Labour History Bulletin*, 25, pp. 5–6, 1972.

17 The very polemic among social historians about the nature of 'social crime' testifies to the importance of the concept. Thus Hobsbawm (ibid.) saw social crime as 'a conscious, almost a political, challenge to the prevailing social and political order and its values'. John Rule, *The Labouring Classes in Early Industrial England, 1750–1850*, Longman, 1979, usefully distinguished between explicit protest crime and crimes tolerated by the masses such as illicit distilling, pillaging wrecks, smuggling, etc. George Rudé, *Criminal and Victim: Crime and Society in Early Nineteenth Century England*, Clarendon Press, 1985, suggested a classification into 'acquisitive crime', 'social' or 'survival' crime and 'protest' crime. Critics of the concept, such as Jim Sharpe, *Crime and Society in Early Modern England 1550–1750*, Longman, 1984, and Clive Emsley, *Crime and Society in England, 1750–1900*, Longman, 1987, generally emphasise the blurred boundaries. Thus 'acquisitive' crime might be a form taken by 'social'

crime or professional organised crime – such as poaching gangs selling to innkeepers – might be involved in 'social' crime, thereby negating the political protest element and placing obstacles in the way of 'determining exactly where social crime ends and normal crime begins' (Sharpe, ibid., p. 140). This debate illustrates fundamental issues of method which cannot be gone into here save to say that the issue is not that of refining conceptual boundaries but rather of grasping the contradictory and dialectical movement of the real historical emergence of the working class.

18 For summary of the debate on the emergence of class consciousness during the late eighteenth century and first half of the nineteenth century, see J. Rule, *The Labouring Classes*, Ch. 16.

19 F. Bovenkerk, 'The Rehabilitation of the Rabble', *Netherlands Journal of Sociology*, no. 20, pp. 13–42, 1984.

20 K. Marx and F. Engels, *Selected Works in One Volume*, Lawrence and Wishart, 1968, p. 44.

21 In the Penguin edition of *Capital* the term 'dangerous classes' is replaced by 'the actual lumpenproletariat'.

22 K. Marx, *Capital*, vol. 1, Foreign Languages Publishing House, 1961, p. 643.

23 Linebaugh, *The London Hanged*, p. 107.

24 C. Emsley, *Crime and Society in England, 1750–1900*, Longman, 1987.

25 V. Gatrell and T. Hadden, 'Criminal Statistics and their Interpretation', in E. Wrigley (ed.), *Nineteenth Century Society*, Oxford University Press, 1972; V. Gatrell, 'The Decline of Theft and Violence in Victorian and Edwardian England', in V. Gatrell, et al. (eds) *Crime and the Law*, Europa Publications, 1982; D. Jones, *Crime, Protest, Community and Police in Nineteenth Century Britain*, Routledge and Kegan Paul, 1982; Emsley, *Crime and Society in England*.

26 'Theory and Evidence of Rising Crime in the Nineteenth Century', *British Journal of Sociology*, no. 33, pp. 404–20, 1982.

27 If this account is true then it stands in ironic contrast to arguments of the 1980s where for some socialists any suggestion of rising crime rates among the poor inner city communities was characterised as an attack on the working class (Lea and Young, *What Is To Be Done?*).

28 G. Stedman Jones, *Outcast London*, Oxford University Press, 1984.

29 M. Savage and A. Miles, *The Remaking of the British Working Class, 1840–1940*, Routledge and Kegan Paul, 1994.

30 B. Lenman and G. Parker, 'The State, the Community and Criminal Law in Early Modern Europe', in V. Gatrell et al., *Crime and the Law*.

31 M. Brodgen, *The Police: Autonomy and Consent*, Academic Press, 1982; 'The Policeman as Domestic Missionary: Urban Discipline and Popular Culture in Northern England, 1850–1880, *Journal of Social History*, IX, 4, 1976.

32 D. Hay, 'Property, Authority and the Criminal Law', in D. Hay (ed.), *Albion's Fatal Tree: Crime and Society in Eighteenth Century England*, Allen Lane, 1975.

33 Though Marx hinted at some of the factors which would secure for capitalism a much longer phase of progressive development than he had initially thought possible. See the discussion in I. Meszaros, *The Power of Ideology*, Harvester Wheatsheaf, 1989, Ch. 7.

34 For a presentation and critical discussion of the evidence, see T. Gurr, 'Historical Trends in Violent Crime: Europe and the United States', in T. Gurr, *Violence in America*, vol. 1, Sage Publications, 1989. For England and Wales during the later nineteenth century, see V. Gatrell, 'The Decline of Theft and Violence in Victorian and Edwardian England', in V. Gatrell, et al. (eds) *Crime and the Law*, Europa Publications, 1980, and for rising crime in the period after 1950, see Lea and Young, *What Is To Be Done?*

35 Lea and Young, *What Is To Be Done?*

36 The separation between the organised drugs economy and more decentralised forms of petty crime is of course artificial, when a high proportion of 'ordinary' burglary, theft and robbery is motivated by the requirements of drug purchasing. See H. Parker et al., *Living with Heroin: The Impact of a Drugs Epidemic on an English Community*, Open University Press, 1988.

37 Hall et al., op. cit., p. 316.

38 According to the *Guardian*, 4 July 1994, among eight pieces of completed Home Office research, whose publication has been postponed or abandoned because their findings fail to support the attitudes of the present Home Secretary, is evidence that Afro-Caribbean youth were less likely to be involved in crime, including drug crime, than their white counterparts.

39 B. Campbell, *Goliath: Britain's Dangerous Places*, Methuen, 1993.

40 Ibid., p. 102.

41 In the form of the 1994 Criminal Justice Act.

5. Engels and Class Consciousness

Cliff Slaughter

SEVEN YEARS AFTER the working class of Russia had made its revolution, Leon Trotsky could say:

> Politics has held the British worker back, has for a long time, so to speak, hobbled him, and he is advancing with such timid, pitiful, MacDonaldite little steps. But when he frees himself from his political trammels, the British racehorse will outstrip our peasant nag.[1]

Clearly, much had happened since Frederick Engels had written, in 1844, in *The Condition of the Working Class in England*, of

> the deep wrath of the whole working class, from Glasgow to London, against the rich, by whom they are systematically plundered and mercilessly left to their fate, a wrath which before too long a time goes by, a time almost within the power of man to predict, must break out into a revolution in comparison with which the French Revolution, and the year 1794, will prove to have been child's play. (4: 323)

How goes the British working class today with this revolution which 'before too long a time goes by ... must break out'? What is the answer to Engels's question: 'What is to become of those destitute millions, who consume today what they earned yesterday; who have created the greatness of England by their inventions and their toil; who become with every passing day more conscious of their might, and demand, with daily increasing urgency, their share of the advantages of society?'

The 'greatness of England' meant the leading economic position of Britain, founded on the solid fact of the birth and ascendancy of industrial capital in that country, with Western European countries and the United States only beginning to follow. Today, Britain is only one, and by no means one of the strongest, of a handful of capitalist 'great powers'. The development of capitalism in Britain, as in all the leading capitalist nations which soon followed in its wake, was to produce a 'national' working-class movement in which, with occasional and minority exceptions, the essentially *international* character of the working class was rejected.

In Britain this process began early, as the capitalist class's advantages of empire and world financial pre-eminence brought rewards which made possible the buying-off of the top layers of the working class and especially of bureaucratic and parliamentary leaders, a phenomenon which became characteristic of all the leading capitalist countries as they entered the imperialist stage of capitalist development in the last years of the nineteenth century. Trotsky noted in 1914 that, long before this, the first 'stormy era of Chartism, of the revolutionary awakening of the British proletariat', at the end of which Engels wrote his book, had given way to another phase:

> The repeal of the Corn Laws (1846), the industrial flowering of the country consequent upon this which turned Britain into the 'workshop of the world', the introduction of the ten-hour working day (1847), the increase in emigration from Ireland to America and finally the extension of the suffrage to the urban workers (1867) were all conditions which significantly improved the position of the upper layers of the proletariat and led its class movement along the peaceful course of trade unionism and the liberal-labour politics that complemented it.[2]

By the turn of the century, the growth of monopoly capital, the merging of industrial and finance-capital, the large-scale export of capital, division of the world between the capitalists of the great powers, then imperialist wars for the division and redivision of the world, the basic features of the imperialist stage, were forming the objective basis upon which the dominant national-reformist parties of the working class consolidated and flourished.

And yet this world-wide expansion of capitalism in its monopoly phase meant at the same time the beginning of a historical period of transition. The concentration and centralisation of capital, the increasing socialisation of production on the international scale, with its growing contradiction between the nation-state and the international division of labour, was a process characterised by ever more marked unevenness of development, which gave rise within individual nations to more and more explosive combinations of the most developed and the most retarded elements of economic, political, cultural and ideological relations. The Russian Revolution of October 1917 was understood by Marxists on this basis. At the very point where proletarian internationalism has suffered its harshest setback, with the German and virtually all other Social-Democratic Parties' endorsement in 1914–18 of their 'own' bourgeoisies' imperialist war, there came the proletarian revolution in Russia. The imperialist chain broke 'at its weakest link' (Lenin). But a heavy price was paid for the opportunist degeneration of the Social Democracy. Its leaders betrayed the revolutions in other countries which followed, particularly in Germany, where the Social Democrats in government actually carried out the bloody counter-revolution of 1918–19.

The struggle of socialists internationally against opportunism and social chauvinism, and then the Russian Revolution, brought the founding of the Third (Communist) International, in which millions of workers came together in new parties on an internationalist programme of socialist revolution. The explicit aim of the leaders of the Communist International was to build a working-class leadership adequate to the theoretical and political tasks of strategy, tactics and organisation in the imperialist period, the epoch of wars and revolutions, of the transition to socialism.

Is this complex history necessary in order to begin to answer Engels's question of three-quarters of a century earlier, what is to become of the working class of England? Yes, because like the international working class as a whole, the British working class became the victim, throughout the rest of the twentieth century, of the consequences of the deadly isolation inflicted on revolutionary Russia. Out of these conditions of isolation and economic and cultural backwardness grew the omnipotence of the machine of bureaucratic control and oppression which found its political expression in Stalinism. By the last weeks of 1924, Stalin and his group controlling the Bolshevik party machine had set a firm course towards delivering that party to the bureaucracy and the virtual merging of party and state apparatus.

The programmatic basis on which this service was rendered was that of 'socialism in one country', borrowed from the armoury of the right wing of that very Social Democracy of Germany which had ensured the arrest of the international socialist revolution on which the fate of Soviet Russia depended. This was the ideological instrument which was to completely 'denature' the communist movement and its essential internationalism. Time and again and in country after country (Britain, China, Spain and others), the working class found itself in struggles which brought to a head the question of state power only to be cruelly betrayed by the Communist Parties and the Soviet bureaucracy, in the early years through gross strategical and tactical mistakes flowing from the theoretical and political degeneration consequent on the line of 'socialism in one country', and soon as a direct consequence of the counter-revolutionary adaptation to imperialism by the Soviet bureaucracy.

This Stalinist destructive work against working-class internationalism reached its acme at the end of the second imperialist world war and the whole subsequent period. In diplomatic and military deals to secure the frontiers of the Soviet Union by creating 'buffer' states in Eastern Europe, at the Yalta and Potsdam conferences, Europe was divided into Soviet and capitalist 'spheres of influence' and military occupation, in which the revolutionary struggles of the armed workers in Italy, France and Greece were sacrificed. Not only were millions of workers and their parties again diverted from revolutionary politics; but capitalism was thereby allowed a breathing space in which the basis was laid for a long period of renewed expanded reproduction. Stalinism adapted to this development with the line of 'peaceful co-existence', 'peaceful, parliamentary roads to socialism', the 'struggle between the two camps', etc.; and the Social Democracy was able in these conditions to achieve a prolonged existence and even a revival, on the basis of Stalinism's discrediting of communism, on the one hand, and of capitalism's renewed ability for some decades to make reform concessions in the advanced countries.

But at the end of the 1980s came a change of incalculable significance: the Stalinist regimes collapsed. They had been undermined by the long-drawn-out crisis of the bureaucratically crippled autarchic 'socialism in one country', no longer able to develop the productive forces once they had reached the stage where creative initiative and management by the freely associated collective were essential, and where the contradictions of a world economy still trapped in the framework of competing nation-states afflicted the Soviet Union just as severely as the capitalist countries. It gradually became not only difficult but impossible to beat down working-class resistance to the demands of the bureaucracy for labour discipline and productivity. The Stalinist regimes had earlier bloodily suppressed the revolutionary uprisings in East Germany (1953), in Hungary and Poland (1956), and in Czechoslovakia (1968). But now they disintegrated ignominiously under the first blows of popular revolt. The Stalinist bureaucracy, with whatever factional groupings and policy differences, has become the direct and open instrument and agency of capitalist restoration, striving itself to be a new capitalist class in these countries, abandoning all claim to represent socialism and the working class.

This is not the place to discuss in detail the consequences of these great changes and the prospects opened up by them. But the study of their implications for the working class, including that of Britain, is a matter of the greatest urgency, and it is from the standpoint of this new situation, to rearm the working class for the new tasks it poses, that we turn again to works like Engels's *The Condition*.

These 'new tasks' are by their nature complex and contradictory. The fight to overcome the national-reformist and Stalinist (socialism in one country) distortion of the class movement of the proletariat can now be carried forward under conditions where the principal barrier between the working class and Marxism for 70 years – Stalinism – is no more. No longer can the many thousands of workers, youth and intellectuals who are thrown forward in every generation in the fight against capitalism be misled by Stalinist parties claiming to be the representatives of a great international movement defending Soviet socialism and the conquests of October. Inevitably a process of differentiation among the forces who had been so misled had begun. The regeneration of Marxism and the reconstruction of the internationalism of the working class, in new and unprecedentedly favourable conditions – this is what confronts the working class today.

Why then characterise the new tasks as 'contradictory'? For two main reasons. First, it goes almost without saying, this overcoming of national-reformist and Stalinist politics in the working-class movement, the reconstruction of proletarian internationalism, must be achieved in the actual practice of building a revolutionary leadership in all the struggles forced upon the working class by imperialism's historical crisis. And these struggles are now inevitably intensifying. Those who thought the collapse of the Stalinist regimes was some kind of victory for capitalism, enabling it through a new expansion to overcome or again displace its contradictions, were wrong. In point of fact, it was the counter-revolutionary politics of the Stalinist bureaucracy in controlling the working class, destroying its internationalism, that constituted capitalism's principal defence. Furthermore, the disintegration of the Stalinist regimes poses not new opportunities but great new problems for world capitalism.

Second, what has become very clear, in the immediate aftermath of the fall of the Stalinist regimes, is the great extent and depth of the damage done to the working-class movement, its class consciousness and organisation, by the long domination of Stalinism. The working-class movement has to be *reconstructed*, and it is necessary to re-study and understand the whole question of revolutionary leadership in this framework, rather than in formal terms of 'providing' an already constructed workers' movement with a new leadership. Those who constitute the vanguard of the reconstruction of the working class must come together in a new revolutionary leadership. Those who have fought for the continuity of Marxism and proletarian internationalism by founding and defending the Fourth International will have to prove themselves in this reconstruction of the class movement of the working class, proving at the same time the indispensability of that continuity, of a definitive reckoning with Stalinism, of the reconstruction of the Fourth International.

We have seen that capitalism is deprived of what has been the main counter-revolutionary force in the workers' movement. Furthermore, capitalism finds its historical crisis as a system (the continued development of which crisis under the surface was the underlying cause of Stalinism's own collapse) exacerbated by the economic, social and political chaos left by the Stalinist regimes' disintegration. And now the accumulated contradictions of capitalism in its imperialist stage, which could be displaced or attenuated for a whole period because of the *political* role of world Stalinism, burst forth with explosive force. Political perspectives and theoretical schemes, which took these long but still temporary and relative adjustments as meaning some sort of new stage of development or some type of equilibrium, were savaged by the eruption of one political explosion or economic crisis after another since the 1960s, and are now useless antiques. The situation now brings home after all the force of the Marxian theory and perspective of permanent revolution:

> In the present epoch ... capitalist development as a whole is faced with insurmountable obstacles and contradictions and beats in frenzy against them. It is precisely this that invests our epoch with its revolutionary character and the revolution with its permanent character.[3]

There is a growing realisation, not only in the working class, that this clash between the needs of capital and the further development of the productive forces which have developed within capitalism itself, has reached a stage which endangers the very survival of nature as we know it, including humanity itself. This is, at a higher level, the contradiction at the heart of capitalism perceived by Engels in 1844 and by Marx. It was starkly expressed 80 years ago by Rosa Luxemburg: 'socialism or barbarism'! Now, at the very point of capitalist production's global extension, the necessity of social ownership and conscious planned control is more clearly than ever a life-and-death matter:

> The system [capitalism] breaks down at the point of its supreme power, for its maximum extension generates the need for restraint and conscious control – and with this, capital production is structurally incompatible.[4]

As the structural crisis now gathers pace, two features of the consequent struggles are particularly marked, and bear directly on the problems of reconstruction and recovery at a new level of the internationalism for which the class movement of the proletariat has had to struggle in its history since Engels's book. First, and for objective reasons which are evident, every working-class struggle today tends to take on immediately an international character; and the successful conduct of such struggles depends on internationalist perspective and programme. And secondly, the working class in recent years has come to face a new situation, in that no reform or trade union struggle can make progress unless it goes beyond the immediate questions and demands it confronts. Even to maintain existing standards, let alone make gains, now requires a radical, revolutionary change in the organisations and the consciousness of the working class, as capital finds itself forced to claw back past working-class gains and concessions, even those which served capital in controlling the working class and diverting its offensive. In every major country, state attack on the trade unions, the basic defence organisations of the working class, is the rule. These are problems forcing upon the working class the necessity to reconstruct its class movement.

Such a 'reconstruction', overcoming (in the dialectical sense of negating, going beyond, carrying forward what is positive) 150 years of its history as a class movement, is obviously a different task from what faced the newly-born working class of 1844. Yet because the problems of the class in 1844 are part of this history which has to be consciously overcome, then those problems, taken up in Engels's book, have to be studied. And a vital part of this study is the study of Engels's own theory and method in the book, its place in the development of Marxist theory as a whole. Thus the *present* and the tasks it poses are the key to the understanding of the past, guiding us to what can be learned from that past to arm us for the tasks of today and tomorrow. Engels's book was written between September 1844 and November 1845. Between September and November 1844, Marx and Engels together wrote a book with a very different title and, at first sight, very different and less 'straightforward' subject-matter: *The Holy Family, or Critique of Critical Criticism (Against Bruno Bauer and Company)*.

This book of essays written separately by Marx and Engels attacked the ideas of the 'Young Hegelian' philosophers around the brothers Edgar and Bruno Bauer. According to them, their own philosophical thinking or 'critical criticism' was the activity which would make history, change the world. Marx and Engels did not content themselves with philosophical and logical arguments against this, nor did they restrict themselves to criticism of the philosophy of Hegel, on which the Bauer brothers claimed to base themselves. The Young Hegelians, having once been radicals, had become active in attacking the idea already advanced by Marx that it is the historical role of the working class to emancipate itself and thereby emancipate all humanity.

The Holy Family, said Engels, is 'a declaration of war' against these 'critical critics', 'who contend that man has nothing to do but to speculate upon metaphysical questions' and who are 'the only important philosophical opponents of Socialism'. Against them, Marx explains the revolutionary role of the working class:

When socialist writers ascribe this world-historic role to the proletariat, it is not at all, as Critical Criticism pretends to believe, because they regard the proletarians as *gods*. Rather the contrary. Since in the fully-formed proletariat the abstraction of all humanity, even of the *semblance* of humanity, is practically complete; since the conditions of life of the proletariat sum up all the conditions of life of society today in their most inhuman form; since man has lost himself in the proletariat, yet at the same time has not only gained theoretical consciousness of that loss, but through urgent, no longer removable, no longer disguisable, absolutely imperative *need* – the practical expression of *necessity* – is driven directly to revolt against this inhumanity, it follows that the proletariat can and must emancipate itself. But it cannot emancipate itself without abolishing the conditions of its own life. It cannot abolish the conditions of its own life without abolishing all the conditions of life of society today which are summed up in its own situation. Not in vain does it go through the stern but steeling school of *labour*. It is not a question of what this or that proletarian, or even the whole proletariat, at the moment *regards* as its aim. It is a question of *what the proletariat is*, and what, in accordance with this *being*, it will historically be compelled to do. Its aim and historical action is visibly and irrevocably foreshadowed in its own life situation as well as in the whole organisation of bourgeois society today. There is no need to explain here that a large part of the English and French proletariat is already *conscious* of its historic task and is constantly working to develop that consciousness into complete clarity. (4: 36–7)

It was this class, and not merely an oppressed and exploited mass, that Engels described in *The Condition*. Before the book was written, not only Marx but also Engels had already perceived the revolutionary role of the working class. Of particular interest is Engels's article, 'The Internal Crises', in the *Rheinische Zeitung* of 10 December 1842:

For although industry makes a country rich, it also creates a class of unpropertied, absolutely poor people, a class which lives from hand to mouth, which multiplies rapidly, and which cannot afterwards be abolished, because it can never acquire stable possession of property. And a third, almost a half, of all English people belong to this class. The slightest stagnation in trade deprives a considerable part of this class of their bread, a large-scale trade crisis leaves the whole class without bread. When such a situation occurs, what is there left for these people to do but to revolt? By its numbers, this class has become the most powerful in England, and woe betide the wealthy Englishmen when it becomes conscious of this fact. So far it is not conscious of the fact. The English proletarian is only just becoming aware of his power. (2: 373)

And Engels goes on to describe the strikes and armed clashes in Yorkshire and Lancashire of the summer of 1842:

> ... unprepared, unorganised and without leadership. The strikers had no definite aim, still less were they united on the nature and method of the action to be taken. Hence, at the slightest resistance on the part of the authorities they became irresolute and unable to overcome their respect for the law. When the Chartists took over the leadership of the movement and proclaimed the People's Charter to the assembled crowds, it was already too late. The only guiding idea vaguely present in the minds of the workers, and of the Chartists as well ... was that of revolution by legal means ... Thus the whole thing fizzled out; every worker returned to work as soon as his savings were used up and he had no more to eat.
>
> However, the dispossessed have gained something useful from these events: the realisation that a revolution by peaceful means is impossible and that only a forcible abolition of the existing unnatural conditions, a radical overthrow of the nobility and industrial aristocracy, can improve the material position of the proletarians. (4: 374)

It is easy to say that the young Engels was over-optimistic in thinking that only a brief experience of strike struggles would bring this 'realisation'. This is still marked in *The Condition*. 'Reviewing the chances of the English bourgeoisie', Engels begins by posing two alternatives: either England is left behind by a more vigorous American capitalism or retains its industrial dominance. In the first case, mass unemployment would leave the English proletariat 'no other choice than to starve or rebel'. In the second, more violent economic crises, growth of the proletariat, concentration of capital and the ruin of the lower middle class would produce a development in which '... there comes a stage at which the proletariat perceives how easily the existing power may be overthrown, and then follows a revolution'. But, says Engels:

> Neither of these supposed conditions may be expected to arise. The commercial crises, the mightiest levers for all independent development of the proletariat, will probably shorten the process, acting in concert with foreign competition and the deepening ruin of the lower middle class. I think the people will not endure more than one more crisis. [The result will be] a revolution with which none hitherto known can be compared. (4: 580–1)

It would not be incorrect to say that *both* these prognoses turned out to be true. For in the period following the writing of *The Condition*,

British capitalism did grow mightily, rapidly, if only for a short period, becoming the workshop of the world. And this growth was inevitably accompanied by a mighty growth of the working class, reflected towards the end of the nineteenth century in, amongst other things, the dramatic growth of trade unionism amongst the unskilled, a development Engels was able to observe and analyse. But, as we know, Britain's monopoly could not last for ever. By the end of the century it was already under heavy pressure and the First World War saw economic and political dominance pass firmly into the hands of American capitalism, as Engels foresaw. This created a situation in which Britain found itself with a powerful, organised, working-class movement, with all the institutions that this involved, but at the same time with an economy less and less able to sustain these conditions.

In the year 1844, it is hardly surprising that no concrete understanding yet existed of how and in what time-scale class-consciousness develops. Marx and Engels undoubtedly already understood what they were to write a short time later in *The German Ideology*, namely, that 'for the success of the cause', a 'mass communist consciousness' was necessary, and that this could come about only through 'the alteration of men on a mass scale', an alteration brought about by their own activity in changing their circumstances. This was the revolution in thought which inspired Engels's book and the activity of Marx and Engels throughout their lives. They were not in the business of predictions, let alone timetables, but of participating in and learning from the revolutionary movement of the working class, and struggling to comprehend all social processes from that standpoint.

In 1844, studying the practice of the English workers, Engels concluded, in a remarkable passage:

> The active resistance of the English working-men has its effect in holding the money-greed of the bourgeoisie within certain limits, and keeping alive the opposition of the workers to the social and political omnipotence of the bourgeoisie, while it compels the admission that something more is needed than Trades Unions and strikes to break the power of the ruling class. (4: 507)

And this should not be read as some sectarian propagandist explanation of 'exposing' the inadequacy of trade unions:

> But what gives these Unions and the strikes arising from them their real importance is this, that they are the first attempt of the workers to abolish competition. They imply the recognition of the fact that the supremacy of the bourgeoisie is based wholly upon the competition of the workers among themselves, i.e., upon their want of cohesion. And precisely because the Unions direct them-

119

selves against the vital nerve of the present social order, however one-sidedly, in however narrow a way, are they so dangerous to this social order. (4: 507)

And a few pages later:

These strikes ... decide nothing, it is true, but they are the strongest proof that the decisive battle between bourgeoisie and proletariat is approaching. They are the military school of the working-men in which they prepare themselves for the great struggle which cannot be avoided; they are the pronunciamentos of single branches of industry that these too have joined the labour movement. (4: 512)

It is interesting to compare this passage with the much later, well-known words of Rosa Luxemburg, explaining that the importance of trade union and parliamentary struggles was that 'in them the working class learns that it is impossible to accomplish a fundamental social change through such struggles, and arrives at the understanding that the conquest of power is inevitable'.

What Engels here explains is a theme consistently held to by himself and Marx throughout their work in the labour movement. They look always for the historical content of what they called the *class movement* of the proletariat, contrasting it with the prescriptions for the development of the working class supplied by the socialist sects of which they were so contemptuous, for example in the First International. The history of the working-class movement has time and time again been bedevilled, and is still, by the strident propagandism of would-be leaders and advisers convinced that the road forward is for correct and logical revolutionary ideas (their own) to get into the heads of more and more workers.

Engels at this very early stage shows how, on the contrary, working-class consciousness is a form – the most decisive form, at this stage of history – of *social* consciousness. It is embodied in and develops through the *class movement*, the organisations, traditions, internal differentiations and relations of the class, and the whole development of the conflict between these and the forces and institutions (political, ideological, economic) of the social order and the ruling class which dominates it. This social consciousness is not simply the aggregate of the individual thoughts of workers; it is not amenable to 'psychology', even 'social psychology', but is understood only on the basis of historical materialism; and socialists can develop the relation between theory and the class-consciousness of the working class as a whole only through practice on that same basis and with that method.

The most direct anticipation, in Engels's writings, of his book was the series of articles 'The Condition of England', published in the

Paris *Vorwarts*, September–October 1844 and written in March of that year. These deal with Thomas Carlyle's *Past and Present*, 'The 18th Century', and 'The English Constitution'. Engels describes the subject-matter of the latter two as 'the condition of England and the essential part of it, the condition of the working class'.

Engels praises to the skies Carlyle's merciless criticism of the emptiness, hypocrisy and brutality of bourgeois England. Yet Carlyle remains unable to take theory and practice beyond this abstract criticism of existing conditions:

> Carlyle recognises the inadequacy of 'competition, demand' and 'supply, Mammonism', etc., and is far removed from asserting the absolute justification of landownership. So why has he not drawn the straightforward conclusion ... and rejected the whole concept of property? How does he think he will destroy 'competition', 'supply and demand', Mammonism, etc., as long as the root of all these things, private property, exists? ... In all Carlyle's rhapsodies, there is not a syllable mentioning the English Socialists. As long as he adheres to his present point of view, which is admittedly far in advance of that of the mass of educated people in England but still abstract and theoretical, he will not be able to view their efforts with particular sympathy. (3: 466)

Carlyle's 'abstract and theoretical' point of view restricted in the same way his view of the struggle of the working class. He could not go beyond sympathy for their rebellion. After the wave of strikes and demonstrations known as the 'Manchester Insurrection' (1842), Carlyle had written:

> A million of hungry operative men ... rose all up, came all out into the streets, and – stood there. What other could they do? Their wrongs and griefs were bitter, insupportable, their rage against the same was just, but who are they that cause these wrongs, who that will ... make effort to redress them? Our enemies are we know not who or what; our friends are we know not where! How shall we attack any one, shoot or be shot by any one? O, if the accursed invisible Nightmare, that is crushing out the life of us and ours, would take a shape; approach us like the Hyrcanian tiger, the Behemoth of Chaos, the Archfiend himself; in any shape that we could see, and fasten on! (cited by Engels 3: 450)

In his comment on this declamation, Engels raises the question of the need for an understanding by the working-class movement of its place in the whole system of bourgeois property and its antagonism to the bourgeois class, as the basis for overcoming the limitations of strikes, revealed so graphically in 1842, a question to which (see above) he returned in *The Condition*:

> But the misfortune of the workers in the summer insurrection of 1842 was precisely that they did not know whom to fight against. The evil they suffered was social – and social evils cannot be abolished as the monarchy or privileges are abolished. Social evils cannot be cured by People's Charters, and the people sensed this – otherwise the People's Charter would be today the basic law of England. Social evils need to be studied and understood, and this the mass of English workers has not yet done up till now. The great achievement of the uprising was that England's most vital question, the question of the final destiny of the working class, was, as Carlyle says, raised in a manner audible to every thinking ear in England. The question can now no longer be evaded. England must answer it or perish. (3: 450)

Carlyle in *Past and Present* wrote a powerful humanist criticism of the soulless world created by capitalism, in which 'cash-payment is the sole relation of human beings'; but there the matter rested, whereas Engels discerns within the disintegration the necessity of humanity's leap to real freedom:

> The disintegration of mankind into a mass of isolated, mutually repelling atoms in itself means the destruction of all corporate, national and indeed of any particular interests and is the last necessary step towards the free and spontaneous association of men. The supremacy of money as the culmination of the process of alienation is an inevitable stage which has to be passed through, if man is to return to himself, as he is now on the verge of doing. (3: 476)

Engels goes on to explain that in England this whole process consists of the thoroughgoing 'social revolution' constituted by the consequences of the abolition of feudalism, and looks forward to the repeal of the Corn Laws and the introduction of the People's Charter, 'in other words, when the aristocracy of birth has been politically overcome by the money aristocracy and the latter in turn by working-class democracy'.

Behind what Carlyle saw, the domination of all human relations by 'self-interest', their replacement by the 'cash nexus', was the industrial revolution. 'This revolution through which British industry has passed,' says Engels, 'is the foundation of every aspect of modern English life, the driving force behind all social development.' But 'the most important effect of the 18th century for England was the creation of the proletariat by the industrial revolution'. And at the end of this series of articles, he opens wide the great question of the struggle for socialism which goes beyond the framework of even the most radical democracy of his day:

> The democracy towards which England is moving is a *social* democracy. But democracy by itself is not capable of curing social ills. Democratic equality is a chimera, the fight of the poor against the rich cannot be fought out on a basis of democracy or indeed of politics as a whole. This stage is only a transition, the last purely political remedy which has still to be tried and from which a new element is bound to develop at once, a principle transcending everything of a political nature. This principle is the principle of socialism. (3: 513)

In *The Condition* Engels returns to Carlyle's *Past and Present*, and to the nature of the working class. Once again, now somewhat more concretely, he sees the motor of change within what Carlyle can see only as human degradation and the collapse of the moral order. Thus Carlyle:

> Revolt, sullen, revengeful humour of revolt against the upper classes, decreasing respect for what their temporal superiors command, decreasing faith for what their spiritual superiors teach, is more and more the universal spirit of the lower classes. Such spirit may be blamed, may be vindicated, but all men must recognise it as extant there, all may know that it is mournful, that unless altered it will be fatal.

Fatal? Engels retorts:

> Carlyle is perfectly right as to the facts and wrong only in censuring the wild rage of the workers against the higher classes. This rage, this passion, is rather the proof that the workers feel the inhumanity of their position, that they refuse to be degraded to the level of brutes, and that they will one day free themselves from servitude to the bourgeoisie. (4: 414)

Engels is certainly no less scathing than Carlyle on the criminal destruction of humanity and culture in the proletariat, their enslavement by the power of money. At the end of the twentieth century, one wonders how those 'sociologists' who have so often (why was it necessary so often?) pronounced the working class extinct, if ever they found themselves compelled to work in industry, would find anything to dispute in Engels's description:

> As voluntary, productive activity is the highest enjoyment known to us, so is compulsory toil the most cruel, degrading punish-

ment. Nothing is more terrible than being constrained to do some one thing every day from morning until night against one's will. And the more a man the worker feels himself, the more hateful must his work be to him, because he feels the constraint, the aimlessness of it for himself. Why does he work? For love of work? From a natural impulse? Not at all! He works for money, for a thing which has nothing whatsoever to do with the work itself; and he works so long, moreover, and in such unbroken monotony, that this alone must make his work a torture in the first weeks if he has the least human feeling left. The division of labour has multiplied the brutalising influences of forced work. In most branches the worker's activity is reduced to some paltry, purely mechanical manipulation, repeated minute after minute, unchanged year after year. (4: 415)

Engels is not concerned only to describe the factory system, any more than, in the same chapter and in his section on 'The Great Towns', he is satisfied to describe the urban chaos created by industrial capitalism. His descriptions are certainly compelling, and have often formed the basis for informed comparison with modern working conditions and urban development, but Engels's subject is the condition of the working class and its development as a class. In the working conditions of wage-slavery

the worker must choose, must either surrender himself to his fate, become a 'good' workman, heed 'faithfully' the interest of the bourgeoisie, in which case he most certainly becomes a brute, or else he must rebel, fight for his manhood to the last, *and this he can only do in the fight against the bourgeoisie.*' (4: 418 emphasis added)

In this sentence is contained the profound truth: bourgeois society, the power of capital, compels the worker to fight to remain a human being, to establish the conditions to develop as a human individual, not by fighting as an individual, against the individual who exploits and destroys his humanity, but *in the fight against the bourgeoisie*; and this fight is the fight of his *class*.

And Engels finds that it is fear of the same *class*-consciousness that strikes fear, and rightly so, in the hearts of the bourgeois critics of living conditions in the great industrial cities:

Dr. Andrew Ure ... tells us that life in the great cities facilitates cabals among the workers and confers power upon the Plebs ... And our bourgeois is perfectly justified in his fears. If the centralisation of population stimulates and develops the property-holding class, it forces the development of the workers yet more rapidly. The workers begin to feel as a class, as a whole; they begin to perceive that, though feeble as individuals, they form a power united; their separation from the bourgeoisie, the development of views peculiar to the workers and corresponding to their position in life, is fostered, the consciousness of oppression awakens, and the workers attain social and political importance. (4: 417–18)

After further elaborating this point, showing how large-scale manufacture and urban concentration had ended the isolation of small groups of workers subjected to their employers, Engels concludes:

In the patriarchal relation that hypocritically concealed the slavery of the worker, the latter must have remained an intellectual zero, totally ignorant of his own interest, a mere private individual. Only when estranged from his employer, when convinced that the sole bond between employer and employee is the bond of pecuniary profit, when the sentimental bond between them, which stood not the slightest test, had wholly fallen away, then only did the worker begin to recognise his own interests and develop independently; then only did he cease to be the slave of the bourgeoisie in his thoughts, feelings, and the expression of his will. And to this end manufacture on a grand scale and in great cities has most largely contributed. (4: 418–19)

One hundred and fifty years after Engels's book, the bourgeoisie is far from looking backwards to any 'patriarchal' relation between employer and worker. In Britain and the other advanced capitalist countries, there were in the intervening years considerable periods during which the bourgeoisie found it possible to contain the organised strength of the working class by dispensing concessions of the 'welfare state' kind. Trotsky went so far as to say that in Britain the capitalists ruled *through* the labour bureaucracy, by means of Labour governments and of the ever-growing tendency of integration of trade unions into the state.

But, as we have already remarked, the stage reached today by the historical, structural crisis of the system imperatively demands the dismantling of this whole mechanism of partial reforms, control and partial integration by the state. This is the basis of the dominant ideological-political forces of the bourgeoisie, and it is echoed faithfully in the Labourites' and Social Democrats' open service to their masters in implementing the consequent policies and openly renouncing even 'reformist' versions of socialism. The working class is now obliged to defend its most elementary rights to organise in trade unions with immunity from the state's use of the forces of law, and its right to strike – those weapons it was only beginning to discover when Engels wrote, and which he explained were so decisive in the development of class consciousness.

Perhaps it constitutes a salutary warning, in the face of the need to go beyond parliamentanianism and defensive trade unionism and turn the universal capitalist attack on policies of 'full employment' and on all the 'welfare' gains of past working-class struggles, to end with Engels's verdict on the Poor Law. It highlights the reactionary nature, in the full sense of the word, of bourgeois politics in today's advanced stage of capitalism's, particularly British capitalism's, decay:

From Newcastle to Dover, there is but one voice among the workers – the voice of hatred against the new law. The bourgeoisie has formulated so clearly in this law its conception of its duties towards the proletariat, that it has been appreciated by the dullest. So frankly, so boldly has the conception never yet been formulated, that the non-possessing class exists solely for the purpose of being exploited, and of starving when the property-holders can no longer make use of it ... In this public measure, in which [the bourgeoisie] acts in its *corpore* as the ruling power, it formulates its real intentions, reveals the animus of those smaller transactions with the proletariat, of which the blame apparently attaches to individuals. And that this measure did not originate with any one section of the bourgeoisie, but enjoys the approval of the whole class is proved by the Parliamentary debates of 1844, ... Thus is the expulsion of the proletariat from State and society outspoken, thus it is publicly proclaimed that proletarians are not human beings, and do not deserve to be treated as such. Let us leave it to the proletarians of the British Empire to reconquer their human rights. (4: 578)

Thus it was, and thus it is. Engels went on to quote an article on the new Poor Law in *The Times* of 7 June 1844: 'War to the mansion, peace to the cottage – is a watchword of terror which may yet ring through the land. Let the wealthy beware!'
The book ends with these words:

This I maintain, the war of the poor against the rich now carried on in detail and indirectly will become direct and universal. It is too late for a peaceful solution. The classes are divided more and more sharply, the spirit of resistance penetrates the workers, the bitterness intensifies, the guerrilla skirmishes become concentrated in more important battles, and soon a slight impulse will suffice to set the avalanche in motion. Then, indeed, will the war-cry resound through the land: 'War to the mansion, peace to the cottage!' – but then it will be too late for the rich to beware. (4: 579)

Notes

1 L. D. Trotsky, *Through what Stage are we Passing?*: speech to the 5th All-Russian Congress of Medical and Veterinary Workers, 21 June 1924.
2 L. D. Trotsky, 'War and the International', November–December 1914; cited in *Trotsky's Writings on Britain*, vol. 1, p. 13.
3 L. D. Trotsky, *The Permanent Revolution*.
4 I. Meszaros, *The Power of Ideology*, Harvester Wheatsheaf, 1989.

6. Engels: A Man of His Time

Peter Fryer

Historical materialism is in a certain sense all there is to Marxism.

– ANTONIO LABRIOLA[1]

Historical materialism both can and must be applied to itself.

– GEORG LUKÁCS[2]

If anything is certain, it is that I myself am not a Marxist.

– KARL MARX[3]

We are bound to say openly what is, and to call a spade – a spade. The working class needs the full truth, however distressing it may be.

– LEON TROTSKY[4]

THE DAY BEFORE Frederick Engels died, Karl Marx's youngest daughter, Eleanor ('Tussy'), travelled up from Sydenham to Regent's Park Road to see him. Samuel Moore, translator of the *Communist Manifesto* of Marx and Engels, and co-translator with Eleanor's husband Edward Aveling of the first volume of Marx's *Capital*, had just told her that Marx was the father of Frederick Demuth, bastard son of Helene Demuth, the Marx family's housekeeper and friend.[5] Unwilling to believe this, since she had always supposed that it was Engels who had fathered Frederick Demuth, Eleanor insisted on hearing the truth from Engels himself. Cancer of the gullet had robbed the 'General' of the power of speech, so he wrote on a slate what she wanted to know. According to Engels's housekeeper, Louise Freyberger, 'Tussy came out so shattered that she ... wept bitterly on my shoulder.' What upset Eleanor was not that Marx had fathered an illegitimate child but that he had disowned the boy, condemning him to a level of education and general culture markedly inferior to her own. Engels commented to Moore: 'Tussy wants to make an idol of her father.'[6]

Unfortunately the disposition to idolise the founders of Marxism has not been confined to Marx's youngest daughter. August Bebel and Eduard Bernstein, first editors of the correspondence of Marx and Engels (1913), and Franz Mehring, author of the first substantial biography of Marx (1918), greatly encouraged the process of idolisation. They did so by erasing entirely, not only all expressions they regarded as vulgar and all references to comparatively trivial personal matters that would have shown the two men in a less than wholly favourable light, but also a large number of politically and ideologically embarrassing statements they had made privately to each other and to third parties. So the world was given a picture of Engels and Marx, and of their thinking on certain matters, that was sanitised and therefore in some respects false.

Engels and Marx were men of their epoch. Their views on the family, on women's place in society, on sexuality, and on related topics, were wholly conventional; on these matters they seem never to have questioned the prevailing assumptions and ideology.[7] More than once Marx expressed disappointment when his wife gave birth to a female child.[8] In a letter written in 1866 to the 24-year-old Paul Lafargue, who had fallen in love with Marx's daughter Laura, then aged 21, Marx showed himself the very model of a Victorian paterfamilias. In its pomposity and patriarchal assumptions, this letter – beginning: 'If you wish to continue your relations with my daughter, you will have to give up your present manner of "courting"' – is typical of many such letters written by Victorian fathers to their daughters' suitors.[9] The barbarism 'homophobia' might have been coined to describe Engels's backward and intolerant views on homosexuality, which he expressed in a letter to Marx in 1869.[10]

More important, Engels and Marx shared another widespread prejudice of their period: an ethnocentrism which saw Europe and the US as spearheading the world's future development and wrote off the inhabitants of the rest of the world as barbarians and savages[11] – though, as will be seen, there is evidence that Marx, at any rate, may have begun to take a rather different view towards the end of his life. For almost all Europeans throughout the nineteenth century, and for long afterwards, ethnocentrism was unquestionable and unquestioned.

'Non-historic' peoples

THE YOUNG ENGELS was an ardent German nationalist, and never completely discarded the nationalist views he held in his youth. In 1841, at the age of 20, he looked forward to the 'Germanisation' of Holland and Belgium, and to a French military defeat in a future Franco-German war. The French, he wrote, held the fixed idea that the Rhine was their property, but to this arrogant demand the only reply worthy of the German nation is Arndt's: 'Give back Alsace and Lorraine!'

For I am of the opinion ... that the reconquest of the German-speaking left bank of the Rhine is a matter of national honour, and that the Germanisation of a disloyal Holland and of Belgium is a political necessity for us. Shall we let the German nationality be completely suppressed in these countries, while the Slavs are rising ever more powerfully in the east? Shall we give up the Germanness of our most beautiful provinces to buy the friendship of France ... ? ... Without doubt, there will be another war between us and France, and then we shall see who is worthy of the left bank of the Rhine.[12]

In the following year, referring to the town of Königsberg, then in Prussia (afterwards Kaliningrad in the USSR), Engels wrote that 'the German element there has rallied its strength and claims to be recognised as German and respected as Germany's representative *vis-à-vis* the barbarism of the Slavonic East'.[13]

By 1848 Engels and Marx had become communists. But that made no difference to their antipathy towards most Slavs. They saw the Slavs, apart from the Poles, as supporters of tsarist reaction in Russia and therefore inherently counter-revolutionary. Early in 1849, in the *Neue Rheinische Zeitung* – a journal subject to Marx's strict editorial control[14] – Engels asserted that among all the large and small nations of the conglomerate then known as Austria, 'only three standard-bearers of progress [the Germans, Poles, and Hungarians] took an active part in history, and still retain their vitality ... Hence they are now revolutionary'. The rest – '[a]ll the other large and small nationalities and peoples' – were 'destined to perish before long in the revolutionary world storm. For that reason they are now counter-revolutionary.'[15] A few paragraphs later there followed his notorious statement about the 'ruined' and 'residual fragments of peoples':

There is no country in Europe which does not have in some corner or other one or several ruined fragments of peoples, the remnant of a former population that was suppressed and held in bondage by the nation which later became the main vehicle of historical development. These relics of a nation mercilessly trampled under foot in the course of history, as Hegel says,[16] these *residual fragments of peoples* always become fanatical standard-bearers of counter-revolution and remain so until their complete extirpation or loss of their national character, just as their whole existence in general is itself a protest against a great historical revolution.

Such, in Scotland, are the Gaels, the supporters of the Stuarts from 1640 to 1745.

Such, in France, are the Bretons, the supporters of the Bourbons from 1792 to 1800.

Such, in Spain, are the Basques, the supporters of Don Carlos.

Such, in Austria, are the pan-Slavist *Southern Slavs*, who are nothing but the residual *fragment of peoples*, resulting from an extremely confused *thousand years of development*. That this residual fragment, which is likewise extremely confused, sees its salvation only in a reversal of the whole European movement ... and that for it the instrument of liberation and the bond of unity is the *Russian knout* – that is the most natural thing in the world.[17]

The Southern Slavs, Engels went on, rose up in 1848 to achieve their national independence only 'in order thereby at the same time to suppress the German-Magyar revolution. They represent the *counter-revolution*'.[18] Engels then ventured a chilling prophecy:

[A]t the first victorious uprising of the French proletariat ... the Austrian Germans and Magyars will be set free and wreak a bloody revenge on the Slav barbarians. The general war which will then break out will smash this Slav Sonderbund [special alliance] and wipe out all these petty hidebound nations, down to their very names.

The next world war will result in the disappearance from the face of the earth not only of reactionary classes and dynasties, but also of entire reactionary peoples. And that, too, is a step forward.[19]

In the following month, attacking 'Democratic Pan-Slavism' in the same journal, Engels elaborated these themes. What, he asked, would have become of these scattered small nationalities, 'which have played such a pitiful role in history', if the Hungarians and Germans had not 'kept them together and led them against the armies of Mohammed and Suleiman' (sultans of Turkey in the fifteenth and seventeenth century respectively)? The Germans and Hungarians united 'all these small, stunted and impotent little nations' into a single big state, thereby enabling them 'to take part in a historical development from which, left to themselves, they would have remained completely aloof!'. Of course, Engels added, 'matters of this kind cannot be accomplished without many a tender national blossom being forcibly broken.[20] But in history nothing is achieved without violence and implacable ruthlessness.'[21] According to Engels:

apart from the Poles, the Russians, and at the most the Turkish Slavs, no Slav people has a future, for the simple reason that all the other Slavs lack the primary historical, geographical, political and industrial conditions for independence and viability.

People which have never had a history of their own, which from the time when they achieved the first, most elementary stage of civilisation already came under foreign sway, or which were *forced* to attain the first stage of civilisation only by means of a foreign yoke, are not viable and will never be able to achieve any kind of independence.

And that has been the fate of the Austrian Slavs. The Czechs, among whom we would include the Moravians and Slovaks ... have never had a history of their own. And this historically absolutely non-existent 'nation' puts forward claims to independence?[22]

Nor had these 'Austrian Slavs' ever had a history of their own: 'from the historical, literary, political, commercial and industrial points of view they are dependent on the Germans and Magyars'. To the 'sentimental phrases about brotherhood' which Bakunin was offering on behalf of 'the most counter-revolutionary nations of Europe', Engels replied with bloodthirsty phrases: '[H]atred of Russians was and still is the *primary revolutionary passion* among Germans; ... since the [1848] revolution hatred of Czechs and Croats has been added, and ... only by the most determined use of terror against these Slav peoples can we, jointly with the Poles and Magyars, safeguard the revolution.' Commenting on Bakunin's promise of a life-and-death struggle until the Slavs had their place in the world, great and free and independent, Engels declared: 'Then there will be a struggle ... against those Slavs who betray the revolution; an annihilating fight and ruthless terror – not in the interests of Germany, but in the interests of the revolution!'[23] There was however a rider:

If at any epoch while they were oppressed the Slavs had begun a *new revolutionary history*, that by itself would have proved their viability. From that moment the revolution would have had an interest in their liberation, and the special interest of the Germans and Magyars would have given way to the greater interests of the European revolution.

Precisely that, however, never happened. The Slavs – once again we remind our readers that here we always exclude the Poles – were always the *main instruments of the counter-revolutionaries*. Oppressed at home, outside their country, wherever Slav influence extended to, they were the *oppressors of all revolutionary nations.*[24]

Far from being simply a youthful aberration on the part of Engels, his low opinion of the 'non-historic' nations was to be repeated several times in later years. In 1852, in a series of articles for an American newspaper (a series republished soon after Engels's death as *Revolution and Counter-Revolution in Germany*), he accused 'the Bohemian and Croatian Panslavists' of having 'betrayed the revolutionary cause for the shadow of a nationality which, in the best of cases, would have shared the fate of the Polish nationality under Russian sway'.[25] The Moravians and Slovaks had long since lost 'every vestige of national feeling and vitality'. The chief champion of the Czech nationality, Professor František Palacký, was 'nothing but a learned German run mad'. But dying Czech nationality – 'dying according to every fact known in history for the last four hundred years' – had made in 1848 a last effort to regain its former vitality. The failure of this effort proved that Bohemia could henceforth exist only as a portion of Germany – 'although part of her inhabitants might yet, for some centuries, continue to speak a non-German language'.[26] These 'dying nationalities, the Bohemians, Carinthians, Dalmatians, &c.' had tried to profit by the universal confusion of 1848 in order to restore their political *status quo* of a thousand years earlier.

> [T]he historical tendency, and at the same time the physical and intellectual power of the German nation to subdue, absorb, and eliminate its ancient eastern neighbours ... this tendency of absorption on the part of the Germans had always been and still was one of the mightiest means by which the civilization of western Europe had been spread in the east of that Continent; ... it could only cease whenever the process of Germanization had reached the frontier of large, compact, unbroken nations, capable of an independent life; ... therefore, the natural and inevitable fate of these dying nations was to allow this progress [i.e. process?] of dissolution and absorption by their stronger neighbours to complete itself.

Could the 'Panslavist dreamers' expect that history

> would retrograde a thousand years in order to please a few phthisical [i.e. consumptive] bodies of men, who in every part of the territory they occupy are interspersed and surrounded by Germans, who from times almost immemorial have had for all purposes of civilization no other language but the German, and who lack the very first conditions of national existence, numbers and compactness of territory?[27]

In 1855 Engels described Slovenians, Bohemians, and Slovaks as mere 'appendages of either the German or the Hungarian nation'. Pan-Slavism had become 'a political programme, with 800,000 bayonets at its service', leaving Europe with the alternatives of subjugation by the Slavs or the permanent destruction of Russia, the centre of their offensive force.[28] Engels returned to the subject in a private letter thirty years later, by which time the list of 'non-historic' nations had grown somewhat longer than it had been in 1849. In a letter to the German socialist leader August Bebel, Engels wrote in 1885 of 'those miserable remnants of what once were nations [*elenden Trümmerstücken ehemaliger Nationen*], the Serbs, Bulgarians, Greeks, and other rapacious riff-raff [*Räubergesindel*], on whose behalf your liberal philistine enthuses in the interests of Russia, are begrudging one another the very air they breathe, and must inevitably slit each other's greedy throats'. And he added: 'It could lead to a situation in which the war machine turns rebellious and refuses to engage in prolonged mutual slaughter for the sake of the lousy [*lausigen*] Balkan nations.'[29]

The most thorough and penetrating analysis of the un-Marxist views of Engels and Marx on the Slavonic peoples – most penetrating, above all, since it criticises them 'from the perspective of their own methodological premises'[30] – is Roman Rosdolsky's *Engels and the 'Nonhistoric' Peoples: The National Question in the Revolution of 1848*, written in 1948 but not published until 1964; it first appeared in English in 1986, in John-Paul Himka's scrupulous English translation. Here their condemnation of the Slavs as for the most part 'non-historic', counter-revolutionary by nature, and doomed to extinction, is attributed to excessive revolutionary optimism. Summarising Rosdolsky's argument, Himka observes that this excessive optimism of Marx and Engels had two fatal consequences:

Firstly, Engels and Marx were unwilling to examine critically their revolutionary allies and too willing to believe only the best about them. Yet these revolutionary allies included, as the sole allies of the revolution in East Central Europe, the Polish and Hungarian *nobility*. These allies oppressed peasants not only of their own nationality, but also of other nationalities – Croatian, Serbian, Ukrainian, Slovak, Romanian. The social protest of the latter peasants naturally took on a national form in 1848. (The situation was similar with regard to the German bourgeoisie in Austria and the Czechs and Slovenes.) Engels closed his eyes to the social side of this protest, which would have impugned the reputation of some crucial allies of the proletariat in 1848, and viewed the protest as exclusively national in content. Secondly, Marx and Engels were expecting the *imminent* collapse of capitalism and the advent of the socialist epoch. Therefore they felt that they could abstract from the social antagonism between landowners and peasants, classes that were about to disappear entirely in the new socialist society.

What Rosdolsky argues, then, is that under the influence of their impatience for the socialist revolution Marx and Engels abandoned, with regard to East Central Europe, a cardinal aspect of their own materialist method: the rigorous *class* analysis of historical phenomena. Unable to come to grips with the *class* contradictions of the revolution, with the *class* basis of the Austrian Slavs' counter-revolutionary conduct, Marx and Engels had to explain that conduct by means of something from outside, 'exoteric' to, their materialist method. They thus reached back into their Hegelian past and made new use of Hegel's altogether idealist conception of 'nonhistoric' peoples to explain the reactionary behaviour of the Austrian Slavs.[31]

Other nationalities

IN GENERAL, MARX and Engels supported national liberation struggles when such struggles seemed to them to be in the long-term interests of the revolution as a whole. But if in their estimation a particular national liberation struggle conflicted with their overall revolutionary aims they never hesitated to oppose it; and on those grounds, as we have just seen, they strenuously opposed the national movements of almost all the Slav peoples of Eastern Europe. They interpreted the long-term interests of the revolution in a very wide sense, supporting various annexations and acts of conquest by bourgeois states that in their view would tend to push to the utmost the democratic revolution against feudalism and autocracy, spread capitalist industry into territories it had not hitherto reached, and foster the emergence of an industrial proletariat. And they never hesitated to take sides vigorously, to the extent of making scathing judgements about nations that they saw as standing in the way of progress. This explains their hostile and derogatory remarks about Danes, Mexicans and the Arab states of North Africa.

In 1848 Engels wrote in the *Neue Rheinische Zeitung* about the German claim on the Danish duchies of Schleswig and Holstein (which Prussia and Austria would eventually take from the Danes in 1864):

The Danish war is the first *revolutionary war* waged by Germany. We therefore *advocated* a resolute conduct of the Danish war from the very beginning ...

The Danish nation is in commercial, industrial, political and literary matters completely dependent on Germany. It is well known that the real capital of Denmark is not Copenhagen but Hamburg; ... and that apart from Holberg, Danish literature is a poor imitation of that of Germany ...

Germany has the satisfaction of knowing that the Scandinavian nations, and especially Denmark, have fallen under her sway, and that compared with *them* she is even revolutionary and progressive ...

By the same right under which France has taken Flanders, Lorraine and Alsace, and will sooner or later take Belgium, with that same right Germany takes over Schleswig; it is the right of civilisation as against barbarism, of progress as against stability ... this right carries more weight than all agreements, for it is the right of historical development.[32]

Two years later Engels declared Denmark to be 'another of these petty states sharing this pride of a national independence and this exorbitant desire to aggrandise themselves'. However:

[t]he independence and power of Denmark ... is [*sic*] of interest to none but Russia and a certain fraction of English politicians ...

The policy of the revolutionary party in all countries has always been to strongly unite the great nationalities hitherto cut up in small states, and to ensure independence and power, not to those small wrecks of nationalities – such as Danes, Croats, Czechs, Slovaks, &c., &c., ... or to those mongrel would-be nations, such as the Swiss and Belgians – but to the large and healthy nationalities now oppressed by the ruling European system. An European confederacy of nations can only be formed by great ... nations ... never by such miserably powerless so-called nations as the Danes, the Belgians, Swiss, &c ...

[T]his war in Schleswig was the only revolutionary war Germany ever carried on. The question was whether the Schleswigers were to be forced to follow the fate of small, impotent, half-civilised Denmark ... or whether they should be allowed to re-unite themselves to a nation of forty millions.[33]

Having 'swotted up the whole question', Engels told Marx towards the end of 1863 that he now thought the German right to Schleswig was confined to the south, 'which is German by nationality and free choice, so that Schleswig would have to be partitioned'. Germany's only chance of liberating the duchies lay in *our starting a war against Russia for the benefit of Poland*. '[T]hen,' he added, 'we could take anything we liked from Denmark with impunity.'[34] After visiting the town of Flensburg in 1864, Engels reported to Marx that the Frisians

regard themselves as a physically and morally superior race to the Danes, and indeed they are ... I have come to the conclusion that the Danes are no more than a nation of advocates, who will *knowingly and brazenly lie*, even in matters of scholarship, if it is in their interest.[35]

Engels regarded the US claim to California in much the same light as the German claim to Schleswig-Holstein. Reviewing 'The

Movements of 1847' early in 1848, Engels observed that 'we have witnessed the conquest of Mexico and have rejoiced at it', adding:

> It is to the interest of its own development that Mexico will in future be placed under the tutelage of the United States. The evolution of the whole of America will profit by the fact that the United States, by the possession of California, obtains command of the Pacific.[36]

He returned to this theme a year later. Was it, he asked rhetorically, 'perhaps unfortunate' that 'splendid California' had been taken away from 'the lazy Mexicans, who could not do anything with it'? Was it unfortunate

> That the energetic Yankees by rapid exploitation of the Californian gold mines will increase the means of circulation, in a few years will concentrate a dense population and extensive trade at the most suitable places in the coast of the Pacific Ocean, create large cities, open up communications by steamship, construct a railway from New York to San Francisco, for the first time really open the Pacific ocean to civilisation, and for the third time in history give world trade a new direction? The 'independence' of a few Spanish Californians and Texans may suffer because of it, in some places 'justice' and other moral principles may be violated; but what does that matter compared to such facts of world-historical significance?[37]

In 1848 Engels likewise hailed 'the conquest of Algeria' by France 18 years before, since it had forced the Beys of Tunis and Tripoli, and even the Emperor of Morocco, 'to enter upon the road of civilisation':

> They were obliged to find other employment for their people than piracy, and other means of filling their exchequer than tributes paid to them by the smaller states of Europe. And if we may regret that the liberty of the Bedouins of the desert has been destroyed, we must not forget that these same Bedouins were a nation of robbers ... All these nations of free barbarians look very proud, noble and glorious at a distance, but only come near them and you will find that they, as well as the more civilised nations, are ruled by the lust of gain, and only employ more and more cruel means.[38]

Jews and the 'Jewish question'

THE REMARKS MADE by the founders of Marxism about Jews and the 'Jewish question' are of two kinds: public and private.

Marx's main public statement 'On the Jewish Question' was written in the autumn of 1843 and published under that title in the *Deutsch-Französische Jahrbücher* in the following year. Thus it dates from early in his career, before he had become a Marxist in the accepted sense. In this review of Bruno Bauer's treatises *Die Judenfrage* ('The Jewish Question', 1843) and 'Die Fähigkeit der heutigen Juden und Christen, frei zu werden' ('The Capacity of Present-Day Jews and Christians to Become Free', 1843), Marx challenged Bauer's view that the social emancipation of the Jews entailed the abolition of the Jewish religion. To Marx this approach, which made religion the cause rather than the effect of social oppression, was philosophical idealism and one-sided. He argued that religion was the manifestation of secular narrowness, not its cause. He characterised the Jews as a religious sect, not a nation. As money-lenders, they had played an important role in the economic life of society since the Middle Ages. Their history had led them to develop many unpleasant traits, all connected in one way or another with the acquisition of money, with huckstering and self-interest. In a future society, where there would be no money and therefore no possibility of making it, these historically determined traits would necessarily disappear. Ultimately the emancipation of the Jews was the emancipation of humanity from Judaism. (It is important to understand that *'Judentum'*, the German word for Judaism, had the secondary meaning of 'commerce', and throughout the article it is this meaning which is uppermost in Marx's mind. The word has for him very little religious content and still less 'racial' content. He uses it to mean, essentially, capitalism.)[39] Without this practical basis of Judaism, 'a general *anti-social* element',[40] Jews as such would cease to exist and there would no longer be any Jewish 'problem'.[41]

This review is the work of a thinker who is poised on the threshold of Marxism but is still a revolutionary democrat and not yet a communist. For the glaring flaw in 'On the Jewish Question' is that it fails to make any distinction between exploited and exploiting Jews.[42] What is missing from it is precisely the proletariat and its role in human emancipation. This next, decisive step in the development of Marxist theory would come a few months after 'On the Jewish Question' was written, in the article called 'Contribution to the Critique of Hegel's Philosophy of Law. Introduction', also published in the *Deutsch-Französische Jahrbücher* in 1844.[43]

In *The Holy Family, or Critique of Critical Criticism* (1845), written in collaboration with Engels, Marx summarised some of the arguments of 'On the Jewish Question' and unequivocally sided with the Jews against Bauer, judging a state's political maturity by the extent to which it has emancipated the Jews.[44] And in the two versions of Marx's 'Theses on Feuerbach' (1845) – both the original version and that edited by Engels – Ludwig Feuerbach's view of the superiority of theory to practice is summed up thus: '[H]e regards the theoretical attitude as the only genuinely human attitude, while practice is conceived and defined only in its dirty-Jewish form of appearance.'[45] Apart from these three early works – and a brief reference in 1854 to 'the misery and the sufferings of the Jews at Jerusalem'[46] – Marx's only other relevant published statement is to be found in *Herr Vogt* (1860), his reply to the slanders of Karl Vogt (1817–95) against himself and the Communist League. Here Marx devotes a long passage to the iniquities of Joseph Moses Levy (1812–88), a founder and the publisher of the *Daily Telegraph*. Much of this passage is occupied with Levy's nose, in terms which must have amused Marx greatly but probably strike most present-day readers as adding nothing to the argument:

> Levy is determined to be an Anglo-Saxon. Therefore, at least once a month he attacks the non-English policies of Mr. Disraeli, for Disraeli, 'the Asiatic mystery', is, unlike the *Telegraph*, not an Anglo-Saxon by descent. But what does it profit Levy to attack Mr. D'Israeli ... when Mother Nature has inscribed his origins in the clearest possible way right in the middle of his face. The nose of the mysterious stranger of Slawkenbergius (see *Tristram Shandy*) who had got the finest nose from the promontory of noses, was just a nine days' wonder in Strasbourg, whereas Levy's nose provides conversation throughout the year in the City of London ... [T]he great skill of Levy's nose consists in its ability to titillate with a rotten smell, to sniff it out a hundred miles away and to attract it. Thus Levy's nose serves the *Daily Telegraph* as elephant's trunk, antenna, lighthouse and telegraph. It is therefore no exaggeration to say that Levy writes his paper with his nose.[47]

There are many references to Jews throughout the almost 40 years of private correspondence between the founders of Marxism, and in letters to third parties by one or other of them, and many of these references are highly scurrilous. Engels writes of 'Jewish swindlers like Disraeli'.[48] Marx gossips rather unpleasantly about the Communist League member Moses Hess.[49] Very unpleasantly, Engels mocks Jewish speech: 'I return Lassalle's letter herewith. Effery eench the puerile Jew.'[50] Ferdinand Lassalle (1825–64), though at first occasionally praised ('Lassalle, despite his many "buts", is *dur* [tough] and energetic';[51] '[a]fter Cluss, Lassalle is by far the most useful of the lot')[52] is far more often criticised. And when they criticise him to each other Engels and Marx seldom forget that he is a Jew, calling him 'Izzy',[53] 'little Jew Braun' and 'His Excellency Ephraim Artful',[54] 'Baron Artful',[55] 'the little Jew',[56] even a 'Jewish nigger'[57] – though Marx is not above trying to borrow money from him,[58] complaining that '[t]he chap would sooner throw money down the drain than lend it to a "friend", even though his interest and capital were guaranteed. In this he bases himself on the view that he ought to live the life of a Jewish baron, or Jew created a baron.'[59] Marx adds:

> It is now quite plain to me – as the shape of his head and the way his hair grows also testify – that he is descended from the negroes who accompanied Moses' flight from Egypt (unless his mother or paternal grandmother interbred with a nigger). Now, this blend of Jewishness and Germanness, on the one hand, and basic negroid stock, on the other, must inevitably give rise to a peculiar product. The fellow's importunity is also niggerlike.[60]

Lassalle was always a man one had to keep 'a devilish sharp eye on', writes Engels,

> and as a real Jew from the Slav border was always [ready?] to exploit anyone for his own private ends on party pretexts. And then his urge to push his way into polite society, ... to disguise the greasy Breslau Jew with all kinds of pomade and paint[,] was always repulsive.[61]

Hearing that Lassalle has been thrown out of a theatre, Engels comments: 'To get himself talked about, I can see the chap keeping someone to give him an annual box on the ears, come the time when his own Jewish effrontery no longer does the trick.'[62] Having visited Lassalle in Berlin, Marx reports to his friend that '[a]t certain times ... *la* Hatzfeldt's voice has a Jewish intonation that has been acquired from and instilled in her by him.'[63] Even long after Lassalle's death in 1864, we find Marx writing to his eldest daughter of his 'cynical, smarmily importunate mannerisms *à la* marquis-cum-Jew'.[64]

Engels tells Marx in 1864: 'Never in my whole life have I had such a glut of Jewish chicanery as now.'[65] Ramsgate, where Marx stays in the summer of 1879, he finds to be 'full of Jews and fleas'.[66] More serious, perhaps, than such remarks is the total silence Marx and Engels seem to have observed, in private as well as in public, about the anti-Jewish pogroms in Russia in the spring of 1881.[67] In itself, this silence proves nothing; but from commentators who otherwise assiduously kept abreast of events, it does suggest a significant blind spot.

DO THEIR PUBLISHED utterances on the 'Jewish question', plus the stream of vituperation that runs for decades through the private correspondence of Engels and Marx, justify the many attempts that have been made to portray them as anti-semites? Rosdolsky writes of these attempts:

> The method is quite simple: one extracts a number of citations from their works and private correspondence, and then one places these citations alongside the concept of anti-Semitism as one understands it (or rather: as the 'sound common-sense' of one's milieu understands it). The result of this uncritical (and thoroughly *unhistorical*) procedure is that ultimately even the founders of Marxism appear to be some sort of spiritual comrades-in-arms of Julius Streicher. Using this method, clearly, it is very easy to put three-quarters of the thinkers, writers and politicians of the past into the camp of anti-Semitism ...[68]

There are four senses of the word 'anti-semitic' which clearly do not apply to the founders of Marxism.

First, Marx and Engels were not anti-semitic in the modern racist sense of considering Jews to be biologically distinct from 'Aryans'[69] and therefore, as Bruno Bauer would in 1863 be one of the first to hold, 'racially' incompatible with the German people.[70]

Second, they were not anti-semitic in a political sense. In March 1843 Marx told his friend Arnold Ruge, the journalist and Young Hegelian philosopher, that he was going to draw up a petition on behalf of the Jewish community in Cologne, on the ground that 'as many breaches as possible' should be made in the Christian state 'in order to smuggle as much as we can of what is rational'.[71] That he supported full political rights for Jews at a time when they did not possess such rights in Germany 'removes Marx at once from the ranks of political antisemites'.[72] To be sure, Engels wrote to Paul Lafargue in 1892: 'I begin to understand French anti-Semitism when I see how many Jews of Polish origin and with German names intrude themselves everywhere, arrogate everything to themselves and push themselves forward everywhere to the point of creating public opinion in the ville lumière [i.e. Paris].'[73] But to claim to understand, or 'begin to understand', is very different from giving political support, and Engels's letter is not inconsistent with his statement of political opposition to anti-semitism, published in a Vienna workers' paper two years earlier:

> Anti-Semitism is the characteristic sign of a backward civilisation and is therefore only found in Prussia and Austria or in Russia. If an attempt at anti-Semitism were made in England or America it

would simply be ridiculed ... Only where there is as yet no strong capitalist class and therefore also no strong wage-earning class, where capital, being still too weak to control the whole national production, has the Stock Exchange as the main scene of its activity, and where production is therefore still in the hands of peasants, landowners, handicraft workers and similar classes surviving from the Middle Ages – only here is capital predominantly Jewish and only here is anti-Semitism to be found ...

Anti-Semitism, therefore, is nothing but the reaction of the mediæval, decadent strata of society against modern society, which essentially consists of wage-earners and capitalists; under a mask of apparent socialism it therefore only serves reactionary ends; it is a variety of feudal socialism and with that we can have nothing to do ...

Added to this, anti-Semitism falsifies the whole position of affairs. It does not even know the Jew it howls down. Otherwise it would know that here in England, and in America ... there are thousands and thousands of *Jewish proletarians*, and that these Jewish workers are in fact the worst exploited and most wretched of all. Here in England we have had *three* strikes of Jewish workers within the last twelve months, and then we are expect to carry on anti-Semitism as a fight against capital?

And apart from this, we owe too much to the Jews. To say nothing of Heine and Börne, Marx was of purest Jewish blood; Lassalle was a Jew. Many of our best people are Jews. My friend Victor Adler, who is at present paying in prison in Vienna for his devotion to the cause of the proletariat, Eduard Bernstein, editor of the London *Sozial-Demokrat*, Paul Singer, one of our best men in the Reichstag – people of whose friendship I am proud, are all Jews! Have I not been turned into a Jew myself by the *Gartenlaube*? And indeed if I had to choose, then rather a Jew than 'Herr *von* ...'![74]

Third, the founders of Marxism, who supported full political rights for Jews, neither sought nor prophesied their extermination, and it is 'absurd to imply, as some writers do, that Marx looked forward to "a world without Jews", as though he espoused their physical extermination'.[75] To base a charge of anti-semitism on Marx's article 'On the Jewish Question', as Julius Carlebach has done, is simply inaccurate.[76] The allegation that 'On the Jewish Question' is anti-semitic can only be supported, argues Hal Draper, 'by reading the attitudes of the second half of the twentieth century back into the language of the 1840s'; it was a contribution, not to anti-semitism, but to 'a hotly fought campaign in favour of Jewish political emancipation'; and the Jewish question that Marx there discussed was 'not the one that dominated the mind of a sick society a century later' but *'For or against the political emancipation of the Jews? For or against equal rights for Jews?'*[77]

Fourth, there is a further sense in which Marx, in particular, must be acquitted of the charge of anti-semitism:

> While to anti-Semites Judaism appears as an innate, immutable attribute of the so-called Jewish race or else as an emanation of a mysterious 'Jewish spirit' (or of the Jewish religion), Marx (in his well-known essay 'On the Jewish Question') seeks to derive the 'Jewish national character' (*Volkscharakter*) of his time from the factual historical role that the Jews played in the economic life of the Middle Ages and the modern period as representatives of merchants' capital. Hence, Judaism for him meant a *social characteristic*, the 'chimerical nationality of the Jew' meant '*the nationality of the merchant, of the man of money in general*' ... This youthful work of Marx's rose high above the flood of anti- and philo-Semitic literature of his time.[78]

Some critics accuse Marx of having a 'Jewish inferiority complex' or a 'renegade psychology' that led him to conceal or compensate for his own Jewish origin by strong and distasteful anti-Jewish attacks.[79] This 'explanation', writes Rosdolsky,

> shifts the focus to an area of only secondary importance for intellectual history. Apart from this, however, the explanation breaks down when confronted with the simple fact that Marx's partner, the non-Jew Engels, had exactly the same position *vis-à-vis* the Jews as Marx had; and moreover, both of them shared their antipathy to the Jews with very many other socialists of the past (including, to mention only a few, Fourier, Proudhon and Bakunin).[80]

Or, as Solomon F. Bloom puts it: 'Although it may appear paradoxical it is fairer to say that Marx absorbed, without much independent reflection, the prevailing prejudice of his time and environment than that he made the Jews the scapegoat of his personal disillusionments and frustrations.'[81] Bloom finds that, if one ranges over Marx's entire contribution,

> the note of internationalism, humanitarianism, and tolerance is found to be unquestionably dominant. Although he disliked many men – perhaps most of the men he met – all his work testified to a deep-rooted and authentic love for mankind. Racial and national oppression seemed no less repugnant to him than any other form of persecution. No nation was regarded as superior or inferior to others. However important certain racial or national tendencies might be, they could not be made the basis for grading human groups hierarchically. Material and cultural achievement was not the final test of human worth. All men were capable of progress.

In assaying Marx's contribution, it is necessary to give a certain weight to the informal expressions of his temperamental personality, but it is essential not to confuse them with the direction of his thought and the quality of his aims.[82]

What Rosdolsky calls 'the deplorable position of the *Neue Rheinische Zeitung* on the Jewish question' was, he says, 'a *children's disease of the workers' movement*. And it was, furthermore, a disorder from which the socialist movement of almost every country suffered.' In fact, only after the Dreyfus affair 'was the peril of anti-Semitism recognized in all its magnitude and unequivocally opposed'.[83]

Irish settlers in England

ENGEL'S *The Condition of the Working-Class in England* (1845), written when its author was 24 years of age, is a famously blistering indictment of capitalism and what it had done to England and the English in the 90 or so years since the start of the industrial revolution. Alike in its picturesque descriptions and its bold analysis of the conditions it describes, this classic text is a masterpiece of social investigation and reportage, much ahead of its time. The psychoanalytically oriented American writer Steven Marcus, who is far from being a Marxist, describes it as a work of intellectual and imaginative vision which includes 'a vision of demoralization and alienation, of the most profound social and personal distress'. Of Engels's account of contemporary Manchester in this book, Marcus writes: 'I know of no representation of an industrial city before this that achieves such an intimate, creative hold upon its living subject.'[84]

But while criticising in this book the 'exaggerated and one-sided condemnation of the Irish national character'[85] contained in Thomas Carlyle's *Chartism* (1839), Engels himself makes observations on the Irish workers in England which seem equally one-sided:

These people having grown up almost without civilisation, accustomed from youth to every sort of privation, rough, intemperate, and improvident, bring all their brutal habits with them among a class of the English population which has, in truth, little inducement to cultivate education and morality ...

These Irishmen ... insinuate themselves everywhere. The worst dwellings are good enough for them; their clothing causes them little trouble, so long as it holds together by a single thread; shoes they know not; their food consists of potatoes and potatoes only; whatever they earn beyond these needs they spend upon drink. What does such a race want with high wages? Whenever a district is distinguished for especial filth and especial ruinousness, the explorer may safely count upon meeting those Celtic faces ... and the singing, aspirate brogue ...

Filth and drunkenness ... they have brought with them. The lack of cleanliness ... which is the Irishman's second nature, becomes terrifying and gravely dangerous through its concentration here in the great cities. The Milesian[86] deposits all garbage and filth before his house door here, as he was accustomed to do at home, and so accumulates the pools and dirt-heaps which disfigure the working-people's quarters and poison the air. He builds a pig-sty against the house wall as he did at home, and if he is prevented from doing this, he lets the pig sleep in the room with himself ... The filth and comfortlessness that prevail in the houses themselves it is impossible to describe. The Irishman is unaccustomed to the presence of furniture ... When he is in want of fuel, everything combustible within his reach, chairs, door-posts, mouldings, flooring, finds its way up the chimney ... [T]he custom of crowding many persons into a single room ... has been chiefly implanted by the Irish immigration. And since the poor devil must have one enjoyment, and society has shut him out of all others, he betakes himself to the drinking of spirits. Drink is the one thing which makes the Irishman's life worth having, drink and his cheery care-free temperament; so he revels in drink to the point of the most bestial drunkenness. The southern facile character of the Irishman, his crudity, which places him but little above the savage, his contempt for all humane enjoyments, in which his very crudeness makes him incapable of sharing, his filth and poverty, all favour drunkenness. The temptation is great, he cannot resist it, and so when he has money he gets rid of it down his throat. What else should he do? How can society blame him when it places him in a position in which he almost of necessity becomes a drunkard; when it leaves him to himself, to his savagery.

[Unskilled occupations] count hordes of Irishmen among their number, and the pressure of this race has done much to depress wages and lower the working-class. And even if the Irish ... should become more civilised, enough of the old habits would cling to them to have a strong, degrading influence upon their English companions in toil, especially in view of the general effect of being surrounded by the Irish. For when, in almost every great city, a fifth or a quarter of the workers, or children of Irish parents, who have grown up among Irish filth, no one can wonder if the life, habits, intelligence, moral stature – in short, the whole character of the working-class assimilates a great part of the Irish characteristics ... [I]t is easy to understand how the degrading position of the English workers ... has been still more degraded by the presence of Irish competition.[87]

'With the Irish,' Engels writes further on, 'feeling and passion predominate; reason must bow before them. Their sensuous, excitable nature prevents reflection and quiet, persevering activity from reaching development.'[88]

In these two passages the young Engels shows no understanding of the forces that had drawn and would continue to draw these settlers across the Irish Sea. He sacrifices depth of analysis and compassion to a glib stereotype. These passages lack the imaginative insight and human sympathy that largely inform the rest of *The Condition of the Working Class in England.*

Black people and 'race'

IN THEIR REFERENCES to black people, Engels and Marx were severely limited by the ignorance and outright racism of the science of their time, which swallowed without question the beliefs of such eighteenth-century charlatans as Samuel Estwick and Edward Long, just as it adopted without question Buffon's use from 1749 of the word 'race' in its zoological connotation.[89] Practically every European scientist and intellectual, throughout the nineteenth century, took it for granted that only white-skinned Europeans were capable of thinking and governing, while other 'races' were inherently inferior. Such views were held by scientists towards whom, for the best of reasons, Marx and Engels had an attitude of deep respect. One such scientist was the great American scholar Lewis Henry Morgan (1818–81), 'Father of American Anthropology' and author of *Ancient Society or Researches in the Lines of Human Progress from Savagery through Barbarism to Civilization* (1877), a book which both Marx and Engels read with great excitement, enthusiasm, and fascination, and from which Marx took copious notes. Engels's *The Origin of the Family, Private Property and the State* (1884), written 'In the Light of the Researches of Lewis H. Morgan', was in part the part-fulfilment of Marx's expressed intention to write a book assessing Morgan's work from the standpoint of historical materialism. It subtracts nothing from Morgan's vast achievement in his own field to acknowledge that Morgan, in his attitude to people of African descent, was an extreme racist. His biographer Carl Resek tells us that:

During the debate in Congress over the Compromise of 1850, Morgan expressed the not uncommon sentiment of Negrophobia, based partially on the belief that the Negro was a separate species. He urged [Senator William Henry] Seward to limit the expansion of slavery because 'it is time to fix some limits to the reproduction of this black race among us. It is limited in the north by the traits of the whites. The black population has no independent vitality among us. In the south while the blacks are property, there can be no assignable limit to their reproduction. It is too thin a race intellectually to be fit to propagate and I am perfectly satisfied from reflection that the feeling towards this race is one of hostility throughout the north. We have no respect for them whatever.'[90]

Nor did Morgan express such racist views only in private. His published writings include the statement that black people were 'feeble in intellect, and inferior in rank to every other portion of the human family'.[91] That Marx and Engels 'failed to dissociate themselves from Morgan's racial views in itself proves nothing',[92] of course; such views were held by a large number of white people in Europe and the US.

It would be wrong however to suppose that Engels and Marx always swallowed such extravagances without question. A case in point is their disparate reaction to a book by the French naturalist Pierre Trémaux (b. 1818), *Origine et transformations de l'Homme et des autres êtres* (1865), advancing the highly crude theory that the nature of the soil determined the nature of the 'racial' type living on it, so that there were as many different 'races' as there were soils of different types. Marx wrote to Engels in 1866 that the author, who had 'spent a long time in Africa', showed 'that the common negro type is only a degeneration of a far higher one'. It was a 'very important work', '[i]n its historical and political applications far more significant and pregnant than Darwin'.[93] Engels did not agree. He reached the conclusion that 'there is nothing to his [i.e. Trémaux's] whole theory because he knows nothing of geology, and is incapable of even the most common-or-garden literary-historical critique'.[94] Marx countered that 'Trémaux's basic idea about the *influence of the soil* ... is, in my opinion, an idea which needs only to be *formulated* to acquire permanent scientific status, and that quite independently of the way Trémaux presents it.'[95] But Engels stuck to his guns: Trémaux's hypothesis sounded 'extremely plausible' and might or might not be correct:

> however, when I see the ridiculous evidence with which Trémaux seeks to substantiate it, ... I cannot but extend the profound suspicions I have of the author of the hypothesis to the hypothesis itself. But when he then goes on to declare that the effect of the soil's greater or lesser age, modified by crossing, is the *sole* cause of change in organic species or races, I see absolutely no reason to go along with the man thus far, on the contrary, I see numerous objections to so doing.[96]

All the same, Engels did seem to believe that some human 'races' had degenerated from 'higher' ones, and that a meat diet had produced larger brains in some human 'races'. These conclusions flow from his brilliant, if flawed, fragment on 'The Part Played by Labour in the Transition from Ape to Man', written in 1876 and included in the posthumously published *Dialectics of Nature*.[97]

By and large, both Engels and Marx habitually slighted black people and their abilities, and this attitude seems to have been based on prejudice. To be sure, Marx wrote, and no doubt sincerely believed, that labour in a white skin could not be free while labour in a black skin was branded; but even on the question of the abolition of slavery Marx did not take the unqualified stand that many have attributed to him. In fact he seems to have believed that the abolition of black slavery was impossible before the slaves had to some degree acquired the slaveowners' culture and language. This is shown by a letter to Engels in 1853 where, discussing a book by the American economist Henry Charles Carey (1793–1879), *The Slave Trade, Domestic and Foreign* (1853), he writes:

The only thing of definite interest in the book is the comparison between Negro slavery as formerly practised by the English in Jamaica and elsewhere, and Negro slavery in the United States. He demonstrates how the main stock of Negroes in Jamaica always consisted of freshly imported barbarians, since their treatment by the English meant that not only the Negro population was not maintained, but also that two-thirds of the yearly imports always went to waste, whereas the present generation of Negroes in America is a native product, more or less Yankeefied, English speaking, etc., and hence *capable of being emancipated*.[98]

It is hard to judge the disparaging comments about the 'racial' characteristics of Paul Lafargue, who was of part-African descent, that are scattered through the letters of Marx and Engels, after as well as before Lafargue became Marx's son-in-law. Was Engels simply being jocular when he wrote to Laura Marx Lafargue in 1887, congratulating her husband on being adopted as candidate for the district known as Le Jardin des Plantes et des Animaux: 'Being, in his quality as a nigger, a degree nearer to the rest of the animal kingdom than the rest of us, he is undoubtedly the most appropriate representative of that district'?[99] There seems to be an affectionate undertone when Marx, in a letter to Laura, refers to Lafargue's 'Creole pate', to which he threatens to administer a 'sound [intellectual] cudgelling' on the subject of Proudhonism.[100] Marx's reference to Lafargue, in a letter to Eleanor, as 'a gorilla offspring' and 'our poor Negrillo' has a completely different ring from the venom he normally splashed on the page when he disliked someone. 'In fact, I liked the boy', he confesses.[101] Telling Engels that his daughter is

148

'half promised to Monsieur Lafargue', Marx describes him as 'my medical Creole' and refers to 'the outbursts of feeling these Creoles are subject to',[102] adding a few weeks later: 'He has a heart of gold but is an *enfant gâté* [spoilt child] and too much a child of nature.'[103] We have already seen how Lafargue's future father-in-law laid down the law to the young man who was courting his daughter; but what is invariably forgotten by those who assert that Marx was a racist[104] is that the couple did marry, apparently without any objection on Marx's part. When later he was cross with his son-in-law, Marx fell back on a convenient 'racial' stereotype: 'Lafargue has the blemish customarily found in the negro tribe – no *sense of shame*, by which I mean shame about making a fool of oneself.'[105] In short, Marx and Engels shared 'the typical attitudes of nineteenth-century Europeans who, regardless of their ideology, thought in terms of a hierarchy of cultures with their own at the top and who occasionally used biology to provide a scientific basis for their categorization of societies into higher and lower forms'.[106]

Like most of their contemporaries, Marx and Engels knew very little about Africa; seem to have totally ignored the Haitian revolution that began in 1791; tended to see non-European societies as possessing no mechanism for social development; and tended to equate modernisation and industrialisation with western culture.[107] All this is undeniable. And yet, 'read in its entirety, Marx's work is a ringing denunciation of imperialism and a devastating denunciation of the West's pretensions to "civilization"'.[108] If mere use of the misleading concept of 'race' is to be the touchstone of racism, then Marx and Engels must be joined in the pillory by countless thousands of writers in the nineteenth and twentieth centuries – so many indeed as to drain the concept of racism of any real significance. In any case, there is now substantial evidence that towards the end of his life Marx was taking an entirely fresh and surprisingly unblinkered look at the non-European peoples whom it was customary in his day to regard as 'primitive', 'uncivilised', 'savages', and 'barbarians'. Franklin Rosemont, who has made a searching and provocative study of Marx's *Ethnological Notebooks*, presents us with a Marx who makes 'vigorous attacks on racism', and a work which, 'unlike anything else in the Marxian canon', fundamentally '[challenges] what has passed for Marxism all these years':

A revolutionist to the end, Marx in 1880 no less than in 1844 envisaged a radically new society founded on a total transformation in human relationships, and sought new ways to help bring this society into being ... In the last couple of years of his life, to a far greater degree than ever before, he focused his attention on people of color, the colonialized, peasants and 'primitives'.

[A]fter reading Morgan ... [h]is entire conception of historical development, and particularly of precapitalist societies, now gained immeasurably in depth and precision. Above all, his introduction to ... tribal societies sharpened his sense of the living *presence* of indigenous peoples in the world, and of their possible role in future revolutions.

Reading Morgan ... added far more than a few stray bits and pieces to Marx's thought – it added *a whole new dimension*.[109]

Unfortunately however Marx seems to have neglected to share his new insights with Engels, who wrote to Kautsky in 1883: 'Those primitive tribes you adduce, with a loose form of monogamy, are, in my view, degenerate, as Bancroft has shown of the Californians of the peninsula.'[110] The authority on whom Engels here relied, Hubert Howe Bancroft (1832–1918), had written of the indigenous population of central and southern California that these 'reptile-like humans' displayed 'bestial laziness', had personal habits 'filthy in the extreme', were 'filthy beyond description', were 'thieving, treacherous, cunning'. And he added: 'they of all men are the lowest'.[111]

THE POLITICAL NEGLECT by Marx and Engels of African-American history and struggles had unfortunate and long-lasting consequences for the socialist movement in the United States. They and their followers showed virtually no interest in black Americans, even in the eventful Reconstruction period that followed the end of the Civil War and the emancipation of four million black slaves in the southern states. The General Council of the International Working Men's Association (First International) invited almost every convention of the US National Labor Union (founded in 1866) to send delegates to its European congresses. But no such invitation was extended to the National Negro Labor Union, founded in December 1869, because black workers in the US were effectively barred from the white labour movement. Its founding convention resolved to send the Revd John Sella Martin, a black Boston clergyman and former anti-slavery campaigner, to attend the 1870 congress of the International. But the General Council did not respond to this overture and seems to have displayed no interest in developing any kind of relationship with black American workers. Its minutes show that it devoted much attention to American affairs but none whatever to the problems of black Americans; and 'neither Marx nor any other member of the General Council bothered to ask why these issues were not discussed'.[112] On 1 November 1870 Marx read to the General Council a long address to the workers of Europe, presented by the International's German and French sections in New York, on the problems facing the American working class. It said nothing about Reconstruction or any other aspect of what was then called the Negro question. That question was simply not an important issue in the minds of Marx or Engels – though at an early stage of the American Civil War Marx had emphasised, in a letter to Engels, and in terms that nowadays would be seen as offensive, what a blow a black regiment in the Northern army would be to Confederacy morale: 'The North will, at last, wage the war in earnest, have recourse to revolutionary methods and overthrow the supremacy of the border slave statesmen. One single nigger regiment would have a remarkable effect on Southern nerves.'[113]

Nor did the 'Negro question' interest Marxists in the US. Both before and after the Workingmen's Party of the USA was formed in 1876, they failed to combat racism within the white American working class.[114] In that year the most influential Marxist in the US, Friedrich Sorge (1827–1906), close friend of Marx and Engels, published the only work he wrote in the English language: *Socialism and the Worker*. This 15-page pamphlet is silent about black workers and their struggles.[115]

It would be wrong to accuse the founders of Marxism of total neglect of the subject. But their references to it are few and far between. Marx writes to Engels in 1877: 'What do you think of the workers of the United States? ... The policy of the new President [Rutherford B. Hayes] will turn the negroes ... into militant allies of the workers.'[116] But in his voluminous correspondence with the leaders of US socialism during the 1880s and early 1890s, Engels seems never once to have mentioned black people, and '[h]is failure to advise American socialists on the Negro question at a time when he was pointing out the weaknesses of their work can only be ascribed to the small importance he attributed to this issue in his evaluation of the American scene'.[117] Neither he nor Marx showed any awareness that the national oppression to which black workers were subjected in the US made them a doubly exploited section of the American working class – nor that white workers in that country enjoyed certain privileges as a result of this super-exploitation of black workers.

The record on this matter of leading European socialists who visited the US was scarcely better. When Wilhelm Liebknecht, Edward Aveling and Eleanor Marx toured the US in 1886 as guests of the Socialist Labor Party they made no reference to the 'Negro question' in any of their published statements; and the Avelings' booklet giving an account of the visit, *The working-class movement in America* (1886), though it contains an entire chapter on 'The Cowboys', finds room for only one passing reference to black people: 'It is also worth noting that the immense coloured population of Kansas is beginning to understand the wage-slavery question.'[118] This 'failure of socialist leadership to express even a passing concern for the problems of black Americans in 1886', writes Foner, contributed to the continued neglect of this issue by the Socialist Labor Party throughout that decade.[119] Though the American socialist pioneer Eugene Debs said the Socialist Party of America, founded in 1901, was 'the black man's hope and friend',[120] and though he and his comrades were described in the African-American press as 'sincere friends' of black people,[121] this party had separate branches for its white and black members in the Southern states.[122] Debs and his comrades showed no special interest in the black question, made no special study of it, and adopted no special programme for black workers. Similarly the first US communists showed no special interest in the question, 'and subordinated it wholly to the general social problem'.[123] There was not a single black delegate at the founding conventions of the US Communist Party and Communist Labor Party in September 1919.[124]

Responsibility for this discreditable record cannot of course be laid entirely at the door of the founders of Marxism. But if they had taken some interest in the history and struggles of black people the record of the American socialist movement in this field after the death of Engels might give cause for pride rather than shame.

Conclusion

THERE ARE TWO ways of looking at Engels and Marx: as infallible church fathers or demigods of some kind; or as the creators of 'a brilliant, but in its deepest essence, thoroughly *critical*, scientific method'.[125] The first way is in fundamental conflict with that very method, and with the reality of the two men's personalities and lives. It distorts Marxism by turning it into a kind of secular religion. That was how Marxism was warped and falsified by Stalinism. Those who prematurely crow over the death of Marxism are celebrating the demise of a caricature that had nothing in common with the method discovered by its founders.

To look at Engels and Marx in the second way means seeing them as they were in reality: fallible human beings, not always consistent or wise in their judgements, liable like everyone else to error and to emotions that sometimes tended to cloud and mislead their thinking. With Marx, years of being dunned by creditors and bailiffs, years of enduring painful carbuncles, digestive disorders and a liver complaint, did little to sweeten his temper or moderate the insults he hurled at those who crossed his path. In their personal weaknesses, as in their inconsistent application of their own method, Marx and Engels were men of their age, representative Victorians in more ways than one.

Their human failings do not vitiate the scientific discoveries they made, nor their immense contributions to human thought. Just as

Newton's fondness for Biblical commentaries does not call in question the law of gravity, so the achievement of Marx and Engels in laying bare the inner workings of capitalist society is untouched by their personal failings and prejudices.[126] In contrast to recent fashionable interpretations of the relation between the personal and the political, Marxism shows how it is possible for a thinker of genius to grasp profound truths about human history without being able to transcend the limitations of the natural sciences of his time. The materialist conception of history is an intellectual conquest wholly independent of the errors, prejudices and shortcomings of the men who first formulated and applied it. So is the theory of socialist revolution and of the role of the proletariat in that revolution. So too is that vision which Marx and Engels were the first to portray in a rational, scientific form – the vision of a future society which will be truly human.

Notes

1 *Socialism and Philosophy*, trans. Ernest Untermann, Charles H. Kerr & Company, 1934, p. 18.

2 *History and Class Consciousness: Studies in Marxist Dialectics*, trans. Rodney Livingstone, Merlin, 1968, p. 228.

3 As quoted in Engels to Eduard Bernstein, 2–3 November 1882; Marx and Engels, *Collected Works*, Lawrence and Wishart, 1975– , vol. 46, p. 356. Cf. Engels to Conrad Schmidt, 5 August 1890; Marx and Engels, *Correspondence 1846–1895: A Selection with Commentary and Notes*, trans. and ed. Dona Torr, Martin Lawrence, 1934, p. 472.

4 'To the Third Congress of the French JSR', *Writings of Leon Trotsky (1936–37)*, 2nd edition, Pathfinder, 1978, p. 300.

5 Helene Demuth was not the 'maidservant' in the Marx household, as Robert Payne calls her in *The Unknown Karl Marx: Documents Concerning Karl Marx*, ed. R. Payne, University of London Press and New York University Press, 1972, pp. 22, 116, 327; nor was she the 'housemaid', as Terrell Carver calls her in *Friedrich Engels: His Life and Thought*, Macmillan, 1989, pp. 163, 164, 165; still less was she the 'chambermaid' of popular legend, as, e.g., Tibor Fischer calls her in *Under the Frog*, Polygon, 1992, p. 77. She was in fact 'never ... looked upon or treated as a servant, but always as one of the family, a sympathetic, understanding friend "in the fullest sense of the term"' (Clara Zetkin to David Ryazonov, 27 February 1929, as summarised and quoted by Yvonne Kapp, 'Frederick Demuth: new evidence from old sources', *Socialist History*, no. 6, Autumn 1994, p. 25; I am grateful to Charlie Pottins for calling this paper to my attention). Kapp adds (p. 27, n. 4) that when Frederick Demuth was conceived, Marx's wife was three months pregnant and may not have been 'entirely unaware of what was going on'. In 1861 Mrs Marx described Helene Demuth as her

'staunch, conscientious companion', adding: 'For sixteen years now she has weathered storm and tempest with us' (Jenny Marx to Louise Weydemeyer, 11 March 1861; 41: 572).

6 Louise Freyberger to August Bebel, 2 September 1898, as quoted in Werner Blumenberg, *Karl Marx: An Illustrated Biography*, trans. Douglas Scott, NLB, 1972, p. 123. Freyberger, Karl Kautsky's first wife, was housekeeper to Engels from December 1890 until his death. Carver, p. 169, thinks this letter is 'very probably inauthentic', but his argument does not carry conviction. Nor do his doubts about Marx having been Frederick Demuth's father, for on this matter '[t]here can be no reasonable doubt' as Yvonne Kapp says in *Eleanor Marx*, Lawrence and Wishart, 1972–76, I, p. 289. Kapp's biography contains (I, pp. 289–97) the best account of Frederick Demuth; it is now valuably supplemented by Kapp, 'Frederick Demuth: New Evidence from Old Sources'; see also Kapp, *Eleanor Marx*, II, p. 597; and Chushichi Tsuzuki, *The Life of Eleanor Marx 1855–1898: A Socialist Tragedy*, Clarendon Press, 1967, pp. 263–4. When she learnt the truth Eleanor lost no time in getting in touch with her half-brother, visited him in Hackney, invited him to her house in Sydenham, and corresponded with him. Her nine surviving letters to him will be found in *The Unknown Karl Marx*, ed. Payne, pp. 327–37.

7 Cf. Gareth Stedman Jones, Foreword to Blumenberg, footnote on p. x.

8 Marx to Engels, 2 April 1851; 38: 324. Marx to Engels, 17 January 1855; 39: 509.

9 Marx to Paul Lafargue, 13 August 1866; 42: 307–9.

10 Engels to Marx, 22 June 1869; 43: 295–6.

11 Cf. Ian Cummins, *Marx, Engels and National Movements*, Croom Helm, 1980, p. 5, referring to their 'fundamentally Eurocentric approach'.

12 Engels, 'Ernst Moritz Arndt', *Telegraph für Deutschland*, no. 5 (January 1841); 2: 149.

13 Engels, 'Marginalia to texts of our time', *Rheinische Zeitung*, no. 145 (25 May 1842); 2: 277.

14 He exercised over the paper what Engels was later to call 'simply the dictatorship of Marx ... a matter of course ... undisputed and willingly recognised by all of us' ('Marx and the *Neue Rheinische Zeitung* (1848–49)', *Der Sozialdemokrat*, no. 11, 13 March 1884; 26: 123).

15 Engels, 'The Magyar Struggle', *Neue Rheinische Zeitung*, no. 194 (13 January 1849); 8: 230. George Watson relies heavily on two flagrant mistranslations in an English rendering of this article when he asserts that Marx and Engels 'advocated racial as well as class extermination' and 'genocide on Socialist grounds' ('The Return of the Sage', *Encounter*, LXXIV/1, January–February 1990, pp. 57–8); cf. the earlier version of which this is a mere réchauffage: *The Idea of Liberalism: Studies for a New Map of Politics*, Macmillan, 1985, pp. 111 ('Marx and Engels ... believed in genocide'), 112 ('Marx and Engels publicly declared that whole nations ... would have to be exterminated under socialism'), 116 ('an act recommended by the socialist scriptures of the nineteenth century: the

mass murder of whole races'), 121 (Marxism was 'the one political doctrine, apart from Bismarckian nationalism, that [Hitler] is known to have studied'), and 163 ('it now looks more than ever likely that the two great massacres of European history were indebted to each other in a technical as well as in an ideological sense, and that in both it was Marxism that led the way'). Watson's source is *Marx and Engels, The Russian Menace to Europe: A Collection of Articles, Speeches, Letters and News Despatches*, ed. Paul W. Blackstock and Bert F. Hoselitz, Allen and Unwin, 1953. As Nicholas Jacobs has pointed out ('Marx, Trash, and Jews', *Encounter*, LXXV/2, September 1990, p. 78), this translation renders *Völkerabfälle* as 'ethnic trash' (p. 63) when 'something more like "redundant remains of peoples" is meant'; and it renders *revolutionäre Weltsturm* ('revolutionary world storm') as 'revolutionary holocaust'.

16 See G. W. F. Hegel, *Philosophy of History*, trans. J. Sibree, P. F. Collier and Son, 1902, pp. 79–80: 'A World-historical individual ... is devoted to the One Aim ... [S]o mighty a form must trample down many an innocent flower – crush to pieces many an object in its path'; and p. 444: the Bulgarians, Serbs, and Albanians were 'left behind as broken barbarian remains in the shocks and counter-shocks of the advancing hordes'. John-Paul Himka points out in his Introduction to Roman Rosdolsky, *Engels and the 'Nonhistoric' Peoples: The National Question in the Revolution of 1848*, trans. and ed. J.-P. Himka, Critique Books, 1986, (special issue of *Critique*), p. 6, that the Hegelian roots of Engels's idea of 'non-historic' peoples were first demonstrated by V[olodymyr]. Levinsky, *L'Internationale socialiste et les peuples opprimés*, Édition du 'Dzvine' (la Cloche), 1920, pp. 5–12.

17 Engels, 'The Magyar Struggle'; 8: 234–5 (emphasis in the original).

18 Engels, 'The Magyar Struggle'; 8: 236 (emphasis in the original).

19 Engels, 'The Magyar Struggle'; 8: 238.

20 A further allusion to Hegel; cf. n. 6 above.

21 Engels, 'Democratic Pan-Slavism', *Neue Rheinische Zeitung*, no. 222 (15 February 1849); 8: 370.

22 Engels, 'Democratic Pan-Slavism'; 8: 367 (emphasis in the original).

23 Engels, 'Democratic Pan-Slavism', *Neue Rheinische Zeitung*, no. 223 (16 February 1849); 8: 371, 378 (emphasis in the original).

24 Engels, 'Democratic Pan-Slavism'; 8: 371–2 (emphasis in the original).

25 Engels, 'Panslavism. The Schleswig-Holstein War', *New-York Daily Tribune*, no. 3,403 (15 March 1852), reprinted in *Revolution and Counter-Revolution in Germany* (1896); 11: 47.

26 Engels, 'Poles, Tschechs and Germans', *New-York Daily Tribune*, no. 3,395 (5 March 1852); 11: 46. František Palacký (1798–1876) wrote, amongst other works, *Geschichte von Böhmen* (Prague, 1836–67), whose five volumes take the history of the Czechs up to the year 1526, when they lost their independence.

27 Engels, 'The restoration of order. Diet and chambers', *New-York Daily Tribune*, no. 3,438 (24 April 1852); 11: 71.

28 Engels, 'Germany and Pan-Slavism', *Neue Oder-Zeitung*, no. 185 (21 April 1855); 14: 157.

29 Engels to Bebel, 17 November 1885; 47: 353–4.

30 Himka, Introduction to Rosdolsky, p. 5.

31 Himka, Introduction to Rosdolsky, pp. 4–5.

32 Engels, 'The Danish-Prussian Armistice', *Neue Rheinische Zeitung*, no. 99 (10 September 1848); 7: 421–3 (emphasis in the original). Ludvig Holberg (1684–1754), born in Norway, settled permanently in Denmark and is regarded as the founder of Scandinavian drama.

33 Engels, 'Letter from Germany. The war in Schleswig-Holstein', *The Democratic Review*, August 1850; 10: 392–4.

34 Engels to Marx, 3 December 1863; 41: 496.

35 Engels to Marx, 2 November 1864; 42: 7–8 (emphasis in the original).

36 Engels, 'The Movements of 1847', *Deutsche-Brüsseler-Zeitung*, no. 7 (23 January 1848); 6: 527. Upper California was ceded by Mexico to the US in 1848 and admitted to the Union in 1850.

37 Engels, 'Democratic Pan-Slavism', *Neue Rheinische Zeitung*, no. 222 (15 February 1849); 8: 365–6.

38 Engels, 'Extraordinary Revelations. – Abd-el-Kader. – Guizot's Foreign Policy', *The Northern Star*, no. 535 (22 January 1848); 6: 471–2.

39 Cf. David McLellan, *Marx before Marxism*, Macmillan, 1970, pp. 141–2, and Solomon F. Bloom, *The World of Nations: A Study of the National Implications in the Work of Karl Marx*, Columbia University Press, 1941, p. 191.

40 Marx, 'On the Jewish Question', *Deutsch-Französische Jahrbücher*, 1844; 3: 170 (emphasis in the original).

41 Marx, 'On the Jewish Question'; 3: 146–74.

42 Cf. Edmund Silberner, 'Was Marx an anti-Semite?', *Historia Judaica*, XI/1, April 1949, p. 24.

43 Marx, 'Contribution to the Critique of Hegel's Philosophy of Law. Introduction'; 3: 175–87.

44 Marx and Engels, *The Holy Family*, 1845; 4: 87–90, 94–9, 106–18.

45 Marx, *Theses on Feuerbach*; 5: 3, 5.

46 Marx, 'Declaration of War – On the history of the Eastern Question', *New-York Daily Tribune*, no. 4,054, 15 April 1854; 13: 107.

47 Marx, *Herr Vogt*, 1860; 17: 245–6. Hafen Slawkenbergius, in Laurence Sterne's *Tristram Shandy*, 1760–67, is the German author of a Latin treatise on noses.

48 Engels to Marx, 24 September 1852; 39: 197.

49 Marx to Engels, 22 September 1856; 40: 69–70.

50 Engels to Marx, 11 May 1857; 40: 129.

51 Marx to Engels, 10 March 1853; 39: 290.

52 Engels to Marx, 11 March 1853; 39: 293. Adolph Cluss (1825–1905), a member of the Communist League, emigrated to the US in 1848 and later abandoned politics.

53 For example, Marx to Engels, 4 February 1860; 41: 26.

54 For example, Engels to Marx, 15 July 1859; 40: 465.
55 For example, Engels to Marx, before 12 August 1862; 41: 404.
56 Marx to Engels, 25 May 1859; 40: 450.
57 Marx to Engels, 30 July 1862; 41: 389. The word 'nigger' is in English in the original.
58 Marx to Engels, 13 September 1854; 39: 481. Marx to Ferdinand Lassalle, 4 April 1859; 40: 411–12.
59 Marx to Engels, 30 July 1862; 41: 389.
60 Marx to Engels, 30 July 1862; 41: 390. The word 'nigger' is in English in the original.
61 Engels to Marx, 7 March 1856; 40: 27.
62 Engels to Marx, c. 25 June 1860; 41: 164–5.
63 Marx to Engels, 7 May 1861; 41: 282.
64 Marx to Jenny Longuet, 11 April 1881; 46: 82.
65 Engels to Marx, 2 November 1864; 42: 6.
66 Marx to Engels, 25 August 1879; 45: 376.
67 Cf. Silberner, p. 50.
68 Rosdolsky, p. 196 (emphasis in the original).
69 Cf. Diane Paul, '"In the interests of civilization": Marxist views of race and culture in the nineteenth century', *Journal of the History of Ideas*, XLII/1, January–March 1981, p. 127.
70 Bruno Bauer, *Das Judenthum in der Fremde*, F. Heinicke, 1863, p. 29.
71 Marx to Arnold Ruge, 13 March 1843; 1: 400.
72 Solomon F. Bloom, 'Karl Marx and the Jews', *Jewish Social Studies*, IV/1, January 1942, p. 6.
73 Engels to Paul Lafargue, 22 July 1892; Frederick Engels, Paul and Laura Lafargue, *Correspondence*, Foreign Languages Publishing House, 1959–[63?], III, p. 184.
74 Engels to an unknown correspondent, 19 April 1890; *Arbeiter-Zeitung*, Vienna, 9 May 1890; Marx and Engels, *Correspondence*, trans. and ed. Torr, pp. 469–71 (emphasis in the original). *Der Sozialdemokrat* was published in London from 1888 to 1890; *Die Gartenlaube* was an illustrated periodical published in Leipzig.
75 Paul, '"In the interests of civilization"', p. 131. Thus, in a pamphlet whose title is an impudent forgery, Dagobert D. Runes, Introduction to Marx, *A World Without Jews*, Wisdom Library, 1959, p. xi, wrote of 'the sanguinary dream of Karl Marx – a world without Jews'.
76 Cf. McLellan, *Marx Before Marxism*, p. 41. Julius Carlebach, *Karl Marx and the Radical Critique of Judaism*, Routledge and Kegan Paul, 1978, p. 357, holds that 'Marx's essay on "Die Fähigkeit" ... must be regarded as an anti-semitic document. It is offensive in its language, untrue, and not only unsupported by any empirical reality but, if anything, is contrary to it. Yet it has been and indeed continues to be damaging and disparaging about a group of people who, through no fault of their own, have become the victims rather than the subject of a supposed radical mythology.'

77 Hal Draper, *Karl Marx's Theory of Revolution*, I, *State and Bureaucracy*, Monthly Review Press, 1977, pp. 591, 604, 608 (emphasis in the original).

78 Rosdolsky, pp. 198–9 (emphasis in the original).

79 See, for instance, Otto Rühle, *Karl Marx: His Life and Work*, trans. Eden and Cedar Paul, Allen and Unwin, 1929, pp. 377–8: 'One may presume that from early childhood he had been on the defensive, earnestly endeavouring, by means of intelligence and industry, to compensate for the disadvantages of birth ... [H]e may ... have felt his descent to entail upon him a social stigma, which must have aroused in him a sense of inferiority ... The reader [of 'On the Jewish Question'] cannot escape the feeling that he ... is demonstratively severing himself from his own race ... But one who takes so much trouble to declare that he is not a Jew must have reason for being afraid of being regarded as a Jew. I think there can be no doubt that this social factor of Marx's Jewish origin intensified his sense of inferiority.' Arnold Künzl, *Karl Marx: Eine Psychographie*, [1966], argues in much the same way, but at considerably greater length.

80 Rosdolsky, p. 197.

81 Bloom, 'Karl Marx and the Jews', p. 16.

82 Bloom, *World of Nations*, p. 195.

83 Rosdolsky, p. 201 (emphasis in the original). For the attitude of socialists to the Dreyfus affair, see George Lichtheim, 'Socialism and the Jews', *Dissent*, XV/4, July–August 1968, pp. 325–7; Jack Jacobs, *On Socialists and 'the Jewish Question' after Marx*, New York University Press, 1992, pp. 15–16.

84 Steven Marcus, *Engels, Manchester, and the Working Class*, Weidenfeld and Nicolson, 1974, pp. 131, 200, 190.

85 Engels, *The Condition of the Working Class in England*, 1845; 4: 390.

86 In using this word as a synonym for 'Irishman' Engels seems to be following Carlyle.

87 Engels, *The Condition of the Working Class in England*; 4: 389–92. For a different translation, see Engels, *The Condition of the Working Class in England*, trans. and ed. W. O. Henderson and W. H. Chaloner, Basil Blackwell, 1958, pp. 104–7.

88 Engels, *The Condition of the Working Class in England*; 4: 560.

89 Cf. Ashley Montagu, *Man's Most Dangerous Myth: The Fallacy of Race*, 5th edition, Oxford University Press, 1974, p. 33. As late as 1857, France's first professor of anthropology relied on Estwick and Long for his view that persons of mixed ethnic origin were infertile; see Armand de Quatrefages, 'Du croisement des races humaines', *Revue des deux mondes*, séconde période VIII (1857), p. 162.

90 Carl Resek, *Lewis Henry Morgan: American Scholar*, University of Chicago Press, 1960, p. 63, n. 21. The Compromise of 1850 provided that California would enter the Union as a free state; that the other territories would be organised without mention of slavery; that Texas would

cede certain lands to New Mexico, and be compensated; that slave-holders would be protected by a strict law on fugitive slaves; and that there would be no slave trade in the District of Columbia.

91 Lewis H. Morgan, *Systems of consanguinity and affinity of the human family*, in *Smithsonian Contributions to Knowledge*, XVII, Smithsonian Institution, 1871, p. 462.

92 Paul, '"In the interests of civilization"', p. 126.

93 Marx to Engels, 7 August 1866; 42: 304–5.

94 Engels to Marx, 2 October 1866; 42: 320. Engels added: 'That stuff about the nigger [in English in the original] Santa Maria and the whites turning into Negroes [a reference to an assertion by a Senegal missionary that black Africans had descended from white people] is enough to make one die of laughing. Especially the idea that the traditions of the Senegal niggers [in English in the original] necessarily deserve credence, *just because these fellows cannot write!*' (emphasis in the original).

95 Marx to Engels, 3 October 1866; 42: 322 (emphasis in the original).

96 Engels to Marx, 5 October 1866; 42: 323 (emphasis in the original). Three days after receiving this letter Marx was recommending Trémaux's book to his friend Kugelmann: 'Although written in a slovenly way, full of geological howlers and seriously deficient in literary-historical criticism, it represents – with all that and all that [in English in the original] – an advance over Darwin' (Marx to Ludwig Kugelmann, 9 October 1866; 42: 327).

97 See *CW*, 25: 452–64. This fragment is remarkable, above all, for its early statement of what much later came to be called environmentalism.

98 Marx to Engels, 14 June 1853; 39: 346 (emphasis in the original). The words 'stock' and 'barbarians' are in English in the original.

99 Engels to Laura Lafargue, 26 April 1887; Frederick Engels, Paul and Laura Lafargue, *Correspondence*, Foreign Languages Publishing House, 1959–[63?], II, p. 37.

100 Marx to Laura Marx, 20 March 1866; 42: 246.

101 Marx to Eleanor Marx, 5 September 1866; 42: 315, 316.

102 Marx to Engels, 7 August 1866; 42: 303–4.

103 Marx to Engels, 23 August 1866, 42: 310.

104 For example, Conway Zirkle, *Evolution, Marxian Biology, and the Social Sciences*, University of Pennsylvania Press, 1959, p. 333 ('Marx and Engels are frankly racists'); and Carlos Moore, 'Were Marx and Engels white racists? The prolet-Aryan outlook of Marxism', *Berkeley Journal of Sociology*, XIX, 1974–75, pp. 125–56.

105 Marx to Engels, 11 November 1882, 46: 374.

106 Paul, '"In the interests of civilization"', p. 138.

107 Cf. Moore, 'Were Marx and Engels white racists?', pp. 126, 139, 146.

108 Jerome M. Himmelstein, 'Marx and Engels are dead: an editorial reply to Carlos Moore', *Berkeley Journal of Sociology*, XIX, 1974–75, p. 158.

109 Franklin Rosemont, 'Karl Marx and the Iroquois', *Arsenal/Surrealist Sub-*

version, 4, Black Swan Press, 1989, pp. 201–10 *passim* (emphasis in the original). I am grateful to Dr James D. Young for calling this important essay to my attention. *The Ethnological Notebooks of Karl Marx*, transcribed and edited by Lawrence Krader, were published at Assen (Holland) by Van Gorcum and Co. in 1972.

110 Engels to Karl Kautsky, 10 February 1883; 46: 437–8.

111 Hubert Howe Bancroft, *The Native Races of the Pacific States of North America*, I, D. Appleton and Company, 1875, pp. 441, 373, 377, 430, 440.

112 Philip S. Foner, *American Socialism and Black Americans: From the Age of Jackson to World War II*, Greenwood Press, 1977; *Contributions in Afro-American and African Studies*, no. 33, pp. 39–40.

113 Marx to Engels, 7 August 1862; 41: 400. The words 'border slave statesmen' and 'nigger regiment' are in English in the original.

114 Cf. Foner, *American Socialism and Black Americans*, p. 42.

115 [F. A. Sorge], *Socialism and the Worker*, printed by J. Weber, 1876. A British edition was published by the Modern Press in 1884, price one penny.

116 Marx to Engels, 25 July 1877, 45: 251.

117 Foner, *American Socialism and Black Americans*, pp. 61–2.

118 Edward and Eleanor Marx Aveling, *The Working-Class Movement in America*, Lowrey and Co., 1888, p. 32.

119 Foner, *American Socialism and Black Americans*, p. 62.

120 *The Voice of the Negro* (Atlanta), June 1904, as quoted in *A Documentary History of the Negro People in the United States*, ed. Herbert Aptheker, Citadel Press, 1951, p. 856.

121 Mary Frances Berry and John W. Blassingame, *Long Memory: The Black Experience in America*, Oxford University Press, 1982, p. 225.

122 Lenin, 'Notebooks on Imperialism', *Collected Works*, XXXIX, Progress Publishers, 1968, p. 591.

123 Cf. Theodore Draper, *American Communism and Soviet Russia: The Formative Period*, Viking Press, 1960, pp. 315–16, 319.

124 Foner, *American Socialism and Black Americans*, p. 305. Not until the Fourth Congress of the Communist International (1922) did leading Marxists recognise, in theses passed unanimously, the importance of 'the Negro problem' as 'a vital question of the world revolution'; see *The Communist International 1919–1943: Documents*, ed. Jane Degras, I (Frank Cass, 1971 reprint), pp. 398–9. The American communists thereafter made 'strident claims of fellowship' with black people but 'failed to survive this test' (James Baldwin, 'Journey to Atlanta', in *The Price of the Ticket: Collected Nonfiction 1948–1985*, Michael Joseph, 1985, p. 21).

125 Rosdolsky, p. 185.

126 Cf. Gareth Stedman Jones, Foreword to Blumenberg, p. xi.

Index

Index by Auriol Griffith-Jones